Drowning in the Clear Pool

Studies in the
Postmodern Theory of Education

Joe L. Kincheloe and Shirley R. Steinberg
General Editors

Vol. 122

PETER LANG
New York • Washington, D.C./Baltimore • Bern
Frankfurt am Main • Berlin • Brussels • Vienna • Oxford

Francis J. Ryan, John J. Sweeder,
& Maryanne R. Bednar

Drowning in the Clear Pool

Cultural Narcissism, Technology, & Character Education

A PRIMER FOR SECONDARY EDUCATION

PETER LANG
New York • Washington, D.C./Baltimore • Bern
Frankfurt am Main • Berlin • Brussels • Vienna • Oxford

Library of Congress Cataloging-in-Publication Data

Ryan, Francis J.
Drowning in the clear pool: cultural narcissism,
technology, & character education—a primer for secondary education /
Francis J. Ryan, John J. Sweeder, Maryanne R. Bednar.
p. cm. — (Counterpoints; Vol. 122)
Includes bibliographical references and index.
1. Moral education (Secondary)—United States. 2. Narcissism in adolescence—
United States. I. Title: Cultural narcissism, technology & character education.
II. Sweeder, John J. III. Bednar, Maryanne R. IV. Title.
V. Counterpoints (New York, N.Y.); vol. 122.
LC311 .R92 373.01'14—dc21 00-048742
ISBN 0-8204-4557-6
ISSN 1058-1634

Die Deutsche Bibliothek-CIP-Einheitsaufnahme

Ryan, Francis J.:
Drowning in the clear pool: cultural narcissism,
technology, & character education—a primer for secondary education /
Francis J. Ryan; John J. Sweeder; Maryanne R. Bednar.
—New York; Washington, D.C./Baltimore; Bern;
Frankfurt am Main; Berlin; Brussels; Vienna; Oxford: Lang.
(Counterpoints; Vol. 122)
ISBN 0-8204-4557-6

Cover painting by: Ivan Beardsley
Name of painting: *Narcissus, 1996.*
60" X 72"
Acrylic on canvas

Cover design by Joni Holst

To Rosina, Bonnie, and Jim

Table of Contents

Preface

April 20, 1999. Columbine High School. Littleton, a comfortable, suburban Colorado community. Twelve students and one teacher killed. The shots heard around the educational world.

In the aftermath of the Columbine tragedy, countless copycat phone threats lit up school office switchboards throughout the country, reminding administrators, students, and parents that no school community was immune from such potential violence. Parents and school officials mobilized, with many calling for metal detectors, aggressive locker searches, and workshops for teachers so that they might be better prepared to identify those students whose public profile — their clothing, music, language, and overall social presentment — might suggest antisocial, violent behavior. Predictably, numerous parents and educators demanded a return to character education, and for those schools with such programs already in place, they insisted on a refinement of strategies that would raise students' moral awareness and that would foster specific prosocial behavior. Many of the character education programs now in schools include conflict resolution techniques and general social coping skills, others derive from values clarification exercises, and still others feature the practicing of clearly defined prosocial attributes such as responsibility and cooperation.

While many of these initiatives may prove helpful in nurturing sound character, as well as the prosocial conduct that should accompany such character, many educators are unaware of recent research in moral development that, when used appropriately in classrooms, can significantly enhance prosocial conduct. This research, which was popularized by William Damon, Jerome Kagan, Edward O. Wilson, and James Q. Wilson, has led to a deeper understanding of how the components of the moral system develop and interpenetrate: self-understanding, social cognition, moral judgment, and moral sentiments. Equally important, research on the prevalence and influence of cultural narcissism, which is marked by ubiquitous displays of self-absorption, grandiosity, feelings of entitlement, and devaluation of others, indicates that those affected by this narcissistic culture, and especially adolescents, would have the normal development of their moral systems seriously compromised. The chapters that follow will examine the moral system, the potentially debilitating effects of cultural narcissism on this system, and the classroom praxis that can nurture the moral system, while simultaneously diminishing the influence of cultural narcissism on adolescent prosocial development.

The book is divided into three parts: "Framework" (chapters 1 through 4), "Praxis" (chapters 5 through 7), and "Afterword." The initial two parts are connected by "Bridge to Praxis." Chapter 1, "Argument," presents the groundwork: the components of the moral system, how the components relate to and nourish each other, and how cultural narcissism, now so prevalent in American life, can sabotage the working of the adolescent moral system. It also includes a brief history of character education, emphasizing how changes in American culture and society impacted on the form and function of various character initiatives in classrooms. Chapter 2, "Cultural Narcissism in American Life," examines the current understanding of cultural vs. clinical narcissism, particularly how child-rearing practices relate to the etiology of the narcissistic syndrome. It also presents the concept of positive narcissism. Chapter 3, "The Moral System and Cultural Narcissism," analyzes in close detail how the components of the moral system—self-understanding, social cognition, moral judgment, and moral sentiments—develop during the elementary and secondary school years. It also examines how elements of cultural narcissism, as exhibited in classroom interaction, can thwart the nurturing of the moral system. Chapter 4, "Cultivating the Moral System through Educational Technology," introduces the concepts of idea and product technologies. It focuses on how a unique blending of these two forms of technology can foster the moral system and mollify the negative effects of cultural narcissism.

"Bridge to Praxis" connects "Framework" to "Praxis." It discusses how generic classroom practices, from instruction to behavioral management to assessment, can be used to nurture the moral system.

The Praxis section examines how character education can be fostered within the curricula of specific academic disciplines. Chapter 5, "Character Education in the English Language Arts Classroom," presents a unit of study focusing on *Hamlet*. Chapter 6, "Character Education in the Social

Studies Classroom," focuses on four curriculum topics: American social history, gender, and identity; geography; historical biography; and multiculturalism, immigration, and identity. Chapter 7, "Character Education in the Mathematics and the Science Classroom," includes a three-to-four day lesson plan using graphic calculators and two-dimensional graphing and presents a biology heredity unit.

Each of the praxis chapters is structurally and pedagogically different, ranging from teaching a full unit to teaching smaller, discrete topics. This variety offers the reader a selection of instructional strategies that integrate content with character education. Most importantly, this variety permits readers to borrow strategies or recommendations from one praxis chapter and to infuse these with strategies from another, resulting in a synergistic model that meets the need of any particular classroom or curriculum.

"Afterword" begins by highlighting the hallmarks of the more effective character-education programs currently in use throughout the United States. It then examines how adults working as scout leaders, coaches, and recreational directors can also nurture moral awareness in adolescents, while addressing the potentially destructive effects of cultural narcissism. This section concludes by presenting an overview of recent explorations into the workings of the emotional and moral brain.

Throughout the book, we have given close attention to gender equity by alternating both masculine and feminine pronouns and proper noun examples. This alternation provides for a more coherent reading and is visually less intrusive that using he/she or s/he.

Acknowledgments

We would like to thank Stephen Andrilli, Associate Professor of Mathematics, and Brother Thomas McPhillips, FSC, Professor of Biology, both of La Salle University. Their guidance and questions were indispensable when we crafted Chapter Seven, Character Education in the Mathematics and the Science Classroom. They patiently reviewed the technical aspects of the lesson activities.

We would also like to thank our undergraduate and graduate students for their thoughtful comments and questions that helped us bring into focus our thesis and praxis activities.

Special acknowledgment is likewise extended to Professors Peter Goldstone and Paul Komisar both of Temple University for introducing Francis Ryan to Christopher Lasch's brilliant analysis of cultural narcissism in American life.

Tremendous gratitude for Ivan Beardsley's permission to use his original painting *Narcissus* (60"x72") as the cover for our book. The painting is featured in a collection at Dragonfly Fine Art Gallery, 2431 Moreno Drive, Los Angeles, CA 90039.

A final note of thanks to LaSalle University for its support during the editing phase of this project.

Abstract

With marked increases in school violence and in related displays of un-
civil, adolescent behavior, educators have been again called upon to generate sustained, focused programs of character education to address these
behaviors. As in the recent past, diversity of community values has rendered such efforts increasingly problematic for many public schools; yet,
a more fundamental impasse to character education has been the rise of
cultural narcissism. Adolescents influenced by an inflated sense of grandiosity, entitlement, devaluation of others, and self-absorption frequently
dismiss character education, and the prosocial behavior on which such
education is based, as irrelevant or constraining to their "me-centered"
lifeplans and belief systems.

To counter the culture of narcissism, classroom teachers need to foster
character education by developing the moral system (self-understanding,
social cognition, moral sentiments, and moral judgment) in each of their
students. They also need to utilize the rich potential of educational technology in nurturing the moral system, while simultaneously diluting the
negative influences of cultural narcissism that pervade so much of contemporary American life.

PART I

FRAMEWORK

Chapter One

Argument

Neil Young's (1994) song "Driveby" includes lyrics that are disturbing not just because they capture the horrid reality that plagues many urban neighborhoods, but also because the title, the term "driveby" itself, is now immediately recognized by almost all Americans. Through print and nonprint news sources, the term has entered our social lexicon, and for many people it stirs no emotion at all. A driveby is just another news event. Repeated accounts of drivebys, as well as drug deals, muggings, and related forms of assault have left many Americans wholly desensitized to the civil and moral grotesqueness that stalks so many of our streets. But such violence is not restricted to the inner cities. Accounts of teenagers shooting each other and even shooting their teachers are also heard in the suburbs and rural America. While most citizens shake their heads in disbelief over such disregard for basic values, laws, and decency, other news accounts contribute to this surrealistic atmosphere that surrounds the darker corners of adolescent subculture, with lurid accounts of the "Prom-Mom" prancing onto the dance floor after delivering her newborn into a toilet, and of other teenagers depositing their newborns into industrial dumpsters. On a less dramatic scale, school children of all ages are vandalizing schools, threatening teachers and administrators, preying on and intimidating their weaker peers, and engaging in a host of other antisocial behaviors inside and outside the classroom on a scale that, in the history of our nation, has never been witnessed before with such regularity and ubiquity.

Against this backdrop of flagrant incivility on the part of many of our youth, social scientists and ethicists have questioned whether our social institutions, and especially our schools, have failed. Damon (1995) anticipated these concerns when he observed that "when vast numbers of young people take to aberrant or attenuated moral pathways in the course of their development, we can be sure that the operative cultural influences are not rousing the full potential of the species" (p. 132).

Educators, too, have questioned how schools in general and teachers in particular, as clear participants within these cultural forces, might better address these ruptures in social conduct. Lickona (1988), Ryan (1986), Wynne (1985–86), and others have called for a return to more direct efforts at character education which focus on the cultivation of specific prosocial behaviors. However, some critics, such as Kohn (1997), are suspicious of the purpose and general direction of character education programs, asserting that these approaches are driven by antiquated assumptions that children are in some ways "broken" and need to be "fixed" (p. 429). At best, says Kohn, such programs "drill students in specific behaviors rather than engage them in deep, critical reflection about ways of behaving" (p. 429).

Other critics claim that character education is fruitless because of the marked socioeconomic, racial, and ethnic diversity of our students in public school, and especially those students in our inner cities. In such climates, these voices argue, consensus on the content and the techniques of engaging in character education is practically impossible. This inability to engage in meaningful character education is further exacerbated in some high schools by the general mayhem and disregard for rules and authority that pervade classrooms, corridors, cafeterias, and playing fields (Kilpatrick, 1992). Such intellectual and philosophical debates may paralyze reasonable efforts to bring any form of character education into the public schools. Yet lost within these debates is the historical point that character education has been an integral part of formal and informal schooling since colonial times. Too often educators today fail to understand how present controversies, educational policies, and classroom practices derive from historical precedent and/or social edicts generated by powerful groups within the dominant culture.

The historical overview that follows examines the social dynamics that gave rise to and shaped the form and function of character education in America from Puritan New England to the present. This overview uses the term *character education* to refer to attempts by teachers, parents, and other authority figures who intentionally cultivate in children specific modes of conduct and the attending habits of mind that undergird such conduct. Moreover, this use of character education includes top-down, deductive approaches to imposing specific values, behavior, and conduct on children as well as bottom-up, inductive approaches that, by reconfiguring the classroom environment, attempt to nurture children's values, behavior, and conduct that, some ethicists claim, are innately within children (Kagan, 1984). Other accounts of how teachers nurture character development through indirect strategies often use the terms *values education* and/or *moral education*. However, for clarity, coherence, and consistency this overview uses the term "character education" as a larger, panoramic concept that includes the general meanings of these two terms. In addition, character education, especially during the past five years, has become the new euphemism for what was previously referred to as moral education (Lockwood, 1997). Finally, by highlighting the similarities, dissimilarities, and contradictions surrounding the purposes and effects of character education over time, this overview provides the necessary context for understanding how present-day cultural narcissism, as a major social force, can thwart character education efforts in the school, the home, and the community.

Character Education in American Culture: Historical Snapshots

Colonial Education: Wrestling with the Devil

While instructional practice and school curriculum have changed dramatically since colonial times, character education has, in various guises, remained a constant component of American education. During the 1630s, the Puritans settled the Massachusetts Bay Colony with the intention of establishing a model society marked by civility, piety, and religion. In the words of the Puritan leader John Winthrop, the settlement was to be "a city upon a hill, [for] the eyes of all people are upon us" (Cremin, 1970, p. 15). To assist in maintaining this civility and religious ethos, the Puritan community enacted the Massachusetts Law of 1642, the earliest colonial example of educational legislation. This law "gave to town officials the power to fine negligent parents and place children in apprenticeships where they could be taught the moral and legal principles of the society as they acquired vocational skills and learned to read and write" (McClellan, 1992, p. 6). Five years later the famous Old Deluder Satan Law expanded the intentions of the earlier law. This 1647 act required any community with at least 50 households to appoint a teacher to provide instruction in reading and writing and any community with 100 or more households to establish a grammar school (Spring, 1986). The grammar school, which today would be similar to an academic high school, would prepare selected boys for higher education, and in so doing would insure that the colony would continue to have educated male leaders capable of preserving Christian values within this new Puritan community (McClellan, 1992).

The Old Deluder Satan Law was so named because it recognized how literacy, specifically literate knowledge of the Bible and other prayer books and religious texts, could buttress a person's will and resolve against the temptations of Satan. And while reading and writing were helpful and even essential for many occupations in the Puritan community, literacy was likewise recognized as crucial for a fuller understanding and appreciation of the nuances and imperatives of religious as well as civil law.

In general, school instruction emphasized readings from *The Bible*, *the Book of Common Prayer*, and the *New England Primer*, this last of which became the mainstay of reading instruction in many of the early colonies. As Spring (1986) observed, this reader clearly captured the religious and authoritarian nature of colonial education. The *Primer* included the alphabet, a guide to spelling, and religious and moral maxims such as, *A wise son makes a glad Father, but a foolish son is the heaviness of his Mother* (Spring, 1986, p. 6). Such maxims are followed by various Protestant prayers and a section entitled "Duty of Children Towards Their Parents." The *New England Primer* ends with the "Shorter Westminster Catechism," included at this point as a capstone question-and-answer activity that was designed to reinforce once more children's relationships to and responsibilities towards their Creator and their fellow believers (Ford, 1962).

Greven, as cited in McClellan (1992), explained that three distinct Protestant religious temperaments influenced character education during the colonial period: the Evangelical Temperament, the Moderate Temperament, and the Genteel Temperament. The first of these emphasized the authoritarian and repressive approach, focusing on humankind's depraved nature and the dictates, through Scripture and tradition, of an austere, demanding Deity. This approach, as captured by the format of the *New England Primer* and its attending pedagogy of memorization, underscored the need to teach children to obey their parents, to restrain their impulses, and to accept the authority of God.

Colonial Americans espousing the Moderate Temperament believed in a more approachable God who lived in a covenant with humanity. They accepted good as well as evil in human nature, and they stressed the control of passion through reason, virtue, and piety by emphasizing duty and industry rather than rigorous self-denial. They sought to guide children's conduct through an amalgam of instruction, affection, and discipline.

Represented by a small but powerful group of colonial elite, the Genteel Temperament reflected a belief in a distant but loving God who demanded little from His earthly charges. Unfettered by the psychosocial tensions of the Evangelical and the Moderate Temperaments, the Genteel fostered free and assertive lifeplans, believing that the Supreme Being would reward them for their virtue and decency. Encouraging some measure of self-assertiveness in their children, they generally refrained from suppressing or controlling their offspring's willfulness; yet, when disciplining was required, they often gave this task to servants, thus maintaining bonds of affection with their children. In short, they approached character education not so much as the shaping of a strict conscience as the cultivation of decorum, respect for the family, and acceptance of duty within their privileged social system (McClellan, 1992).

All three temperaments influenced the direction and configuration of character education in colonial America; however, the fostering of character shifted dramatically from the Puritan Commonwealth in Massachusetts through the Declaration of Independence. "Seventeenth-century Americans tended to follow the rigorous approaches of the Evangelicals while eighteenth-century Americans became increasingly moderate in their approaches. Genteel approaches were never widespread but were more common in the late colonial era than in the early years when a distinct gentleman class had not yet developed" (McClellan, 1992, p. 5).

The Early Republic: Fashioning Republican Machines

Education has frequently been summoned by political philosophers, writers, and educators to preserve the principles of all major revolutions, and this was clearly the case after the Revolutionary War and the ratification of the Constitution. With democracy in place, the Founding Fathers of the new nation called for schools to safeguard the tenets of democracy through the cultivation of a new *American Identity*, a sociocultural personality. Such cultivation would necessarily involve character education, which would erect the scaffolding for this type of democratic personality. One of the most vocal supporters of the school's role in the shaping of character was Benjamin Rush, the foremost physician in the new republic.

Receiving his medical education at the University of Edinburgh, considered then to provide the most advanced medical training in Europe, Rush believed in the Enlightenment precept that the plight of humankind could be improved through various social institutions, including schools. He also advocated that such schooling was critical in developing nationalism and in balancing freedom and order (Spring, 1986). Human improvement and nationalism were the pistons that drove Rush's arguments for education in general and for character education in particular.

Rush was a proponent of faculty psychology, which posited that the human mind was segmented into discrete parts, such as intelligence and morality. One common feature of the numerous understandings of faculty psychology was the belief that virtuous functioning of the moral faculty is dependent on how it is cultivated. "For instance, the prescription given by Rush for a well-functioning moral faculty included sunshine, a plain diet, water, and cleanliness. Rush also included with these physical remedies 'mechanical means of promoting virtue,' such as odors, eloquence from the pulpit, music, and solitude" (Spring, 1986, p. 49).

In terms of schooling, Rush maintained that public schools should impose on children a system of values that would create what he called Republican Machines. One of the first major American educational theorists to argue for the superiority of the public schools over the family, he asserted: "Let our pupil be taught that he does not belong to himself, but that he is public property . . . but let him be taught at the same time that he must foresake and even forget them when the welfare of his country requires it" (Spring, 1986, p. 34). Rush argued that the social order of the new nation depended on the control exerted over the student in school. He captured here a shift in the locus of character education from the Puritan pronouncement of obedience to authority based on Divine precept to the Republican pronouncement that such obedience should support democracy and social stability. Despite the apparent secularizing of Puritan motives for respecting parents and elders, Rush's perspectives on character education contained residual elements of the Puritan consciousness. To illustrate, he observed that the most useful citizens were formed from those youths who "have never known or felt their own wills till they were one and twenty years of age" (Spring, 1986, p. 35). Rush implied here a recognition of human growth and development and the freedom and incipient maturity that accompanies young adulthood, yet his emphasis on restraining the will recalls the Evangelical Temperament of the early Puritans. Rush (as cited in Rudolph, 1965) underscored his belief in the essential and constraining influence of religion in the formation of character by noting that

> it is necessary to impose upon them [youth] the doctrines and discipline of a
> particular church. Man is naturally an ungovernable animal, and observation on

particular societies and countries will teach us that when we add the restraints of ecclesiastical to those of domestic and civil government, we produce the highest degree of order and virtue. (p. 12)

During the same time that Benjamin Rush was arguing for the creation of Republican Machines, Noah Webster was busy working on several school books, a speller, a grammar, a reader, and a dictionary, designed to foster a common American culture. Webster contended that the United States, in breaking politically from England, needed to develop its own unique culture; one of the seminal tools in such a development was a common language. Echoing Rush's sentiments regarding national unity, Webster asserted that "a national language is a bond of national union" (Commager, 1962, p. 6). To this end, Webster compiled his famous *Dictionary,* which codified American spelling and pronunciation. He also published the *American Spelling Book* which, like his dictionary, emphasized common American rhetoric. The speller, also referred to as the "Blue-Backed Speller," contained brief stories that emphasized American values, such as hard work, diligence, compassion, helpfulness, and fairness. The speller also included "Precepts Concerning the Social Relations," a short guide suggesting ways for children and young adults to maneuver through social discourse and interaction. Here again, Webster infused these passages with proper American conduct and character. For instance, he recommended that a prospective husband look for a woman who has "softness of manners," "modest deportment," "an accomplished mind and religion," and "a love for domestic life." But he should reject any woman "devoted to dress and amusement," who "delighted with her own praise," and was "an admirer of her own beauty." Continuing to generate this repository of prescribed social values and conduct, Webster directed a prospective wife to reject a suitor who is "a gambler," "a tipler," "a haunter of taverns," and "above all, a scoffer at religion" (Commager, 1962, pp. 93–94). These precepts proselytized correct conduct and character for parents, brothers, sisters, sons, daughters, and, as a constellation of behaviors, the precepts supplemented the values reflected in the speller's short fiction.

Early versions of the *American Spelling Book* contained a Federal Catechism, whose inclusion imitated the format of the earlier *New England Primer*. Interestingly, the Federal Catechism articulated differences between a democracy and a republic, and it emphasized the merits of the new republican government, as well as each student's responsibility for participating as an active citizen within the republic. Webster's books influenced early education in the nineteenth century beyond measure, focusing on the tools of literacy and the moral strengths and values of the new nation. And like Rush, Webster maintained that character education needed to be imposed on students by adults: "Good republicans . . . are formed by a singular machinery in the body politic, which takes the child as soon as he can speak, checks his natural independence and passions, makes him subordinate to superior age, to the laws of the state, to town and parochial institutions" (Warfel, 1936, p. 335).

The National Period: Horace Mann and the Common School

The Common School Movement, which began during the first half of the nineteenth century, established the bedrock on which contemporary public schools are built. Beginning in the 1830s and 1840s and extending through midcentury, common schools appeared first in the East and gradually moved westward. These schools were publicly funded and were controlled, as a system, by local and state governments. These schools influenced the professionalization of teachers as well as the growth of normal schools, which were developed specifically for training teachers. The concept of the common school was championed by Horace Mann, secretary of education in Massachusetts from 1837 to 1849. He believed that "Common Schools . . . shall create a more far-reaching intelligence and a purer morality than has ever existed among communities of men" (Cremin, 1957, p. 7). In many ways the common schools, which were initially an elementary school phenomenon, extended those types of character education espoused by Rush and Webster. Like these educators, Mann believed that a common culture, reflected in a common curriculum for all children and reinforced by a common value system, was essential for preserving the republican form of government established by the Founding Fathers. He was equally aware that the increasing cultural and religious diversity of the nation might threaten attempts to foster a common culture. As Cremin (1957) explained: "Fearing the destructive possibilities of religious, political, and class discord, Mann sought a common value system which might undergird American republicanism and within which a healthy diversity might thrive" (p. 8).

The core values of the common school, like those illustrated earlier in Webster's textbooks, reflected the native Protestant ideology, which stressed "unity, restraint, self-sacrifice, and the careful exercise of religion" (Kaestle, 1983, p. 8). These values were clearly and coherently depicted in various school books used in the common schools, but they were vividly portrayed in the *McGuffey Reader*, the seminal text of character education from the 1840s through the early nineteenth century.

Prepared specifically by William Holmes McGuffey during the 1830s for use in the common schools, the McGuffey Readers revealed a range of moral values and the different expectations for boys and girls in dealing with moral issues (Spring, 1986, p. 141). For example, McGuffey's 1843 *Newly Revised Eclectic Second Reader* contained 104 readings from one to three pages, and about 35% of these focused squarely on the nurturing of specific character traits. Of these didactic stories, 29 addressed character development in boys and just 8 emphasized character formation in girls. This disproportion proceeded in part from society's belief in the moral superiority of females (Burstyn, 1984). Nevertheless, girls were admonished in these stories for overeating, untidiness, and lack of appreciation for learning, the last of which is ironic considering the lack of educational opportunity for most females during those years.

For boys, a recurrent theme was the male relationship with nature, which was both a reinforcement of the male stereotype as active (Sroufe, Cooper, & DeHart, 1996) and as agents for responsibly developing the frontier of the new nation (Spring, 1986). Yet, boys were also encouraged to value learning and to practice charity, honesty, courage, and industriousness, while deploring gluttony, alcoholism, envy, and insolence (Spring, 1986). The cultivation of these traits was encouraged not only to provide for a stable, republican society based on adherence to law, but also to forge a collective personality well-suited for productive participation in America's rapidly expanding industries. Referred to as industrial virtues (Bowles & Gintis, 1976), many character traits such as honesty, industriousness, punctuality, and deference to authority embodied the attitudes of the ideal nineteenth-century factory worker.

While the *McGuffey Reader* was the centerpiece of character education in classrooms during these years, other texts were often used, either as supplements to the *McGuffey* or alone, to foster and reinforce proper conduct. For example, grammar books listed adages on industry, such as "It often requires days digging to obtain pure water," "The path to fame is altogether an uphill road," and "Idleness is the nest in which mischief lays its eggs." In Wilson's *Third Reader*, the "industrious boy is happy and prosperous," while the "idle boy is almost invariably poor and miserable" (Kaestle, 1983, p. 83). Such aphorisms on the benefits of industry recognize that poverty could be rectified by personal effort. "Hard-working people in temporary poverty caused by personal calamity deserved charity; but those unworthy individuals whose chronic poverty was caused by indolence deserved their plight. Their children, of course, had to be rescued and taught that industry was a central trait of the virtuous individual" (Kaestle, 1983, pp. 82–83).

These observations regarding nineteenth-century social and economic relations ironically anticipate perspectives and debates surrounding social welfare programs in present-day America; however, they also capture the Enlightenment belief in the improvability of humankind. A corollary to this belief was the Calvinistic perspective held by many Protestants that wealth was a sign of the Deity's approval, and poverty a sign of disapproval. In this context, for the poor to achieve wealth, they had to be industrious, virtuous, and religious, and for the rich to continue to receive God's blessings, they had to use their wealth in godly ways. This paradigm led to the belief that charity was a means for the well-to-do to remain worthy of their wealth in God's eyes, as well as a justification for a concentration of such wealth in their families (Spring, 1986).

One of the most salient features of character education during the early and mid-nineteenth century was its continued emphasis on preparing students for participation in an industrialized, republican, and essentially Protestant culture. And like earlier efforts, such character education was top-down or deductive. In many ways, it assumed a consensus of values within communities, values that were to be imposed by adults, and especially by teachers, on younger children. There was little if any provision in classrooms for examining the ethical fine points of these values. Instead, children were drilled through reading and writing exercises to appreciate and understand the rewards and punishments for practicing or failing to practice these virtues and behaviors.

The Progressive Period: Dewey and His Critics

From the late nineteenth century through World War II, two competing forms of character education dominated public schools: the progressive approach and the direct character approach. Progressivism as an educational phenomenon was "a many-sided effort to use the schools to improve the lives of individuals" (Cremin, 1964, p. viii). Specifically, it focused on three elements of the educational enterprise: a broader school program to include health, hygiene, and the quality of family and community life; second, the use of child-centered pedagogy derived from the new research from the social sciences, especially from psychology; and third, the development of curriculum and instruction to meet the needs and interests of the increasing kinds and classes of children who were attending the public schools (Cremin, 1964).

While numerous educators have been associated with progressivism, John Dewey has had the most enduring and dramatic influence on the shape and function of the movement. Pedagogically, Dewey refined the group-oriented instruction of Francis Wayland Parker, who, as superintendent of public schools in Quincy, Massachusetts, in the late nineteenth century, contended that the schoolroom should foster both cooperation and democracy. Dewey endorsed the use of cooperative learning groups as part of his project method of teaching. He believed that children must experience cooperation in the classroom if they are to live cooperatively in society and to practice democratic living. These cooperative classroom experiences should not only reinforce rationale problem solving skills, but they should also engender in students empathy and respect for various points of view (Johnson & Johnson, 1991). Dewey's pedagogy organically interfaced with his understanding of character development. While he did not deny the character-building potential of modeling the behavior of virtuous teachers (Tanner, 1997), he believed that character education was not an enterprise separate from the student activities that occurred daily in the classroom. For Dewey, the social and the moral were one (Tanner, 1997).

Dewey explained these linkages in many of his works, but in *Democracy and Education* (1916), he provided a full account of the interpenetration of the social with the moral, and in so doing, he framed this interplay against the backdrop of top-down character education programs that had largely dominated the public school classroom throughout the nineteenth century. As he pointed out:

> Moral education in school is practically hopeless when we set up the development of character as a supreme end, and at the same time treat the acquiring of knowledge and the development of understanding, which of necessity occupy the chief part of school time, as having nothing to do with character. On such a basis, moral education is inevitably reduced to some kind of catechetical instruction, or lessons about morals. Lessons 'about morals' signify . . . lessons in what other people think about virtues and duties. . . . It increases dependence upon others, and throws upon those in authority the responsibility for conduct. (p. 354)

Here, Dewey indicted character education approaches that required students to engage in catechetical instruction similar to that found in the *New England Primer*, in Webster's *American Spelling Book*, and in the *McGuffey Reader*. Instead, Dewey advocated that the classroom be reconfigured to provide children opportunities to practice moral conduct. Through cooperative learning, children would work together on projects, the social interaction of which would naturally foster character traits such as "[o]pen-mindedness, single-mindedness, sincerity, breadth of outlook, thoroughness, [and] assumption of responsibility for developing the consequences of ideas [all of] which are accepted . . . moral traits" (Dewey, 1916, pp. 356–357).

Dewey recognized that truthfulness, honesty, chastity, and related virtues stood out as being patently moral, but he likewise maintained that the prosocial dimensions of human conduct, which were nurtured through cooperative learning, were also moral. On this point, he asserted that educators have frequently defined moral conduct too narrowly,

> giving, then, on one side, a sentimental goody-goody turn without reference to effective ability to do what is socially needed. . . . Morals concern nothing less than the whole character, and the whole character is identical with the man in all his concrete make-up and manifestations. To possess virtue does not signify to have cultivated a few namable and exclusive traits; it means to be fully and adequately what one is capable of becoming through association with others in all the offices of life. (Dewey, 1916, p. 357)

Dewey's model of character education relies on a bottom-up inductive approach (Chazan, 1985). This student-centered process, in expanding traditional understandings of the moral, placed the child in classroom situations which, because of the social interaction, would lead to moral awareness, moral thinking, and, ideally, to moral conduct. As Dewey concisely observed, "All education which develops the power to share effectively in social life is moral" (1916, p. 360).

As a group, progressive educators expected social learning to teach democratic decision making, to help children to break from tradition, and to create their own novel solutions to moral problems. As Hartshorne and May noted (cited in McClellan, 1992), in progressive education those life situations that derived "from the experiences of children in the group . . . are discussed not in terms of some preformulated code but in terms of the problems confronted, or the efforts made to solve these problems, of the success or failure met with, and of the principle of conduct suggested by the total experiences" (p. 64).

Critics of the progressive approach argued that by denigrating tradition, confronting adult authority, and providing legitimacy to peer influence, such strategies rendered children vulnerable to the tyranny of both the immediate group and the present moment (McClellan, 1992). In addition, many teachers found it nearly impossible to provide character education that had no place for particular virtues: "To teach a process of thinking without specific content was a challenge many could simply not meet" (McClellan, 1992, p. 66). Addressing the practical and theoretical shortcomings of progressive methods of character education, Hutchins (1917) and other like-minded educators argued for a return to specific character content or virtues that should be taught directly to children in the public school classroom. Those who favored this direct approach "sought not to turn back the clock but rather to master the new era, to create programs of moral education that would prepare people to cooperate under the altered circumstance of the twentieth century without losing their integrity and without falling victim to the worst temptations of the day" (McClellan, 1992, p. 56). What distinguished these educators from the progressives was their reliance on character codes. Influenced by the character codes of the Boy Scouts, Campfire Girls, and 4-H Clubs, such codes listed specific virtues, frequently packaged as laws or pledges, which were designed to provide focus for character education outside as well as inside the school (McClellan, 1992). One of the most influential codes was the *Children's Morality Code*, authored and published by William Hutchins in 1917. The code listed ten laws of right living and included the following: self-control, good health, kindness, sportsmanship, self-reliance, duty, reliability, truth, good workmanship, and teamwork (Hutchins, 1917). Used in its complete form or modified to meet the intentions of specific communities, Hutchins's code was adopted by many public schools throughout the country. For instance, during the 1920s and 1930s Boston schools added a law of obedience, which became the backbone of their character education program. Schools in Birmingham, Alabama highlighted one virtue each year beginning with first grade, thereby completing their entire 12-part code by grade twelve (McClellan, 1992). Character codes were designed to provide adult guidance and specific virtues which, critics claimed, were lacking in progressive programs of character education. Ironically, proponents of character codes frequently advocated judicious use of many progressive instructional practices in their programs. While nineteenth-century teachers tended to perceive the classroom as a collection of individual students who learned moral principles through contact with textbooks and teachers, these twentieth-century character educators stressed the importance of group dynamics in the classroom. "Impressed both by the importance of teamwork in modern forms of production and by the new psychological theories about the formation of social instincts, these educators expected group interaction to play a vital role in developing character" (McClellan, 1992, p. 58). In short, these educators activated the force of peer influence to foster character development but without ever giving up their own authority in the classroom.

Character educators also used these virtues to generate themes for classroom posters, guides for corridor conduct, templates for extracurricular

behavior, and of course as outlines for classroom instruction. The pervasiveness of these virtues saturated students at every turn within the school
day. This saturation was, according to proponents, essential for motivating students towards prosocial moral conduct. Despite their being influenced by recent scholarship in child psychology, many of these educators
perceived character education as essentially an issue of motivation, not of
moral judgment. They therefore utilized various strategies to engender
moral habits of mind and to fortify the will of students against temptation.
For these teachers, the essential focus of character education was having
the strength to follow prescribed behavior rather than the ability to recognize and analyze fine points within ethical dilemmas (McClellan, 1992).

These two views, the progressive approach and the direct character
approach, influenced most character education efforts during the first half
of the twentieth century. Schools generally used one approach or the
other, while other schools crafted models that drew from each. After
World War II, several national and international events dramatically altered the position and configuration of character education in most public
schools throughout the nation.

The Postwar Period: Moral Thinking
and the New Relativism

The 1960s thrust American society, and especially the public schools,
into moral dilemmas that rendered character education problematic. Efforts to achieve racial equality, protests over the Vietnam War, deepening
cultural pluralism, and a growing tendency to loosen the range of acceptable personal conduct challenged educators to find a common ground,
and especially a commonly held list of behaviors on which to base character education programs (McClellan, 1992). Educators tended to back away
from earlier codes which, to many communities, seemed hypocritical,
authoritative, and constraining. Yet teachers recognized that ethical issues continued to pervade the daily business of classroom instruction,
and that questions of value could not be ignored if they were serious
about preparing students for the world of work, for higher education, and
for participation in a democratic society. Faced with these realities, many
teachers turned to Simon, Howe, and Kirschenbaum's (1972) values clarification approach and/or to Kohlberg's (1970) cognitive developmentalist
approach to character education.

Simon et al. (1972) argued that students needed to develop their own
system of values, particularly because of the moral contradictions and
confusion that pervaded American culture during the late 1960s. Simon
and his colleagues offered values clarification as an antidote for this moral

complexity. Instead of emphasizing specific character content in the class-room, values clarification stressed a seven-step valuing process: "1, priz-ing and cherishing; 2, publicly affirming; 3, choosing from alternatives; 4, choosing after consideration of consequences; 5, choosing freely; 6, act-ing; 7, acting with pattern, consistency, and repetition" (Simon et al., 1972, p. 19). Simon explained that values clarification, in training stu-dents to use this valuing process, would help them become aware of the beliefs and behavior that they cherished and ideally provide them the confidence and resolve to act upon these beliefs. In *Values Clarification: A Handbook for Practical Strategies for Teachers and Students*, Simon, Howe, and Kirschenbaum (1972) presented numerous activities appro-priately fitted to various adolescent and young adult age groups, which were designed to foster this seven-step process, thereby raising student sensitivity to the role of values in their lives.

Like Simon and his associates, Kohlberg (1970) believed that teachers should guide students to a heightened awareness of moral thinking, not just instill in them specific conduct, which he denigrated as "a bag of virtues" (p. 59). Commenting on this process, he asserted that "the teach-ing of virtue is the asking of questions and the pointing of the way, not the giving of answers. Moral education is the leading of men upward, not the putting into the mind knowledge that was not there before" (Kohlberg, 1970, p. 58).

Deriving much of his model from Piaget's (1965) theory of moral de-velopment, Kohlberg hypothesized that human moral development un-folds through three levels, each with two stages: "Preconventional Moral-ity (Stage 1: Punishment-Obedience Orientation; Stage 2: Instrumental Relativist Orientation); Conventional Morality (Stage 3: Good-Boy—Nice Girl Orientation; Stage 4: Law and Order Orientation); Postconventional or Principled Orientation (Stage 5: Social Contract Orientation; Stage 6: Universal Ethic Principle Orientation)" (Biehler & Snowman, 1993, p. 78). Kohlberg claimed that by examining a person's response to moral dilemmas, the person's moral level could be inferred, discussed, and re-fined. Within the classroom, a teacher could enhance moral development through large and small group discussion which permitted students to analyze their own moral thinking and then to reevaluate their own think-ing by examining it in relation to others (Eggen & Kauchak, 1992). Ide-ally, students would be able to refine their own moral thinking and tran-scend to higher levels of moral understanding.

Kohlberg's model has been criticized by Gilligan (1982), who argued that his research more accurately reflected the moral development of male adolescents rather than female adolescents. Other critics, however, indicted both Simon and Kohlberg for developing moral paradigms that, while apparently accommodating the increasing pluralism of the public school classroom, did not provide students the moral guidance they needed. Sommers (1984) pointed out that values clarification is strong on process but short on substance. Recalling some of the earlier criticism directed at progressivism, Sommers maintained that values clarification is contentless. In guiding students to identify what and why they value certain people, objects, and events, values clarification teachers, in remaining themselves morally neutral by not commenting on student discourse, failed to separate the truly moral from the trivial. In such classrooms, "Children are queried about their views on homemade Christmas gifts, people who wear wigs, and whether or not they approve of abortion or would turn in a hit-and-run driver as if no significant differences existed among these issues" (Sommers, 1984, p. 383). Sommers also faulted Kohlberg and his followers for their attempts at developing in schools and classrooms *just communities* that are based on moral dialogues between peers and where teacher input is minimized. Also finding weaknesses in Kohlberg's model, others feared that the heavy emphasis on moral discussion ignored the issues of motivation and resulted in a form of "rhetorical sophistication" that gave students the ability to rationalize their actions without inspiring them to behave in principled ways (McClellan, 1992, p. 94).

Despite the controversy surrounding values clarification and cognitive development theory, both perspectives are critical to understanding the evolution of character education in American school culture because together they have positioned moral thinking at the center of the debate. And this repositioning of moral thinking influenced many of the character education programs that gained popularity throughout the 1980s and 1990s.

During the 1980s and 1990s, character education evolved into two general ideological camps. Reacting to the alleged contentlessness of Simon's and Kohlberg's respective approaches, the resurgence of the direct character education approach, with its philosophical connections to Hutchins's (1917) earlier model, appeared in many public schools. Headquartered in San Antonio, Texas, the American for Character Education Institute developed a practical, useful, and workable method to teach character, conduct, and citizenship in elementary schools. This program was organized around *Freedom's Code*, which emphasized

> being honest, generous, just, kind, and helpful; having courage and convictions along with tolerance of the views of others; making good use of time and talents; providing security for self and dependents; understanding and fulfilling the obli-

gations of citizenship; standing for truth; and defending basic human rights under
the law. (McClellan, 1992, p. 97)

Freedom's Code made its way into various education kits, filmstrips, transparencies, and textbooks. Moreover, teachers were encouraged to use
multimodal pedagogy, such as simulations, role-playing, stories, discussions, projects, and case studies, as a way of introducing and reinforcing
these core virtues. *Freedom's Code* was designed to be infused into the
English language arts or the social studies curriculum, or it could stand
alone in the school day, with five to ten minutes given to young children
and longer periods given to adolescents (McClellan, 1992). This direct
approach to character education was endorsed by Bennett (1992), who
insisted that specific values should be taught in public schools: "It is by
exposing our children to good character and inviting its imitation that we
transmit to them a moral foundation. This happens when teachers and
principals, by their words and actions, embody sound convictions"
(p. 58).

In addition to the direct approach to character education, several hybrid approaches appeared during the 1980s and 1990s which blended
the emphasis on moral reasoning and student-centered pedagogies of the
1960s with the virtues of the direct approach. For example, Bennigna
(1988) maintained that teachers should use direct as well as indirect strategies to foster justice, persistence, generosity, loyalty, social cooperation,
and fairness. These attributes are "important and deserve emphasis in
the curriculum, whether we achieve that emphasis by praising students
for demonstrating accepted values, by having them follow rules that embody those values, or by encouraging them to emulate heroes from history and literature" (p. 418).

One of the most influential spokespersons for a hybrid approach to
character education is Lickona. Drawing from the research of Erikson,
Piaget, and Kohlberg, Lickona (1988) identified three broad goals of character development. These included the combating of egocentrism and
individualism, the fostering of moral awareness, and the construction of a
moral school community based on fairness, caring, and participation.
"Such a community [would be] a moral end in itself, as well as a support
system for the character development of each individual student" (p. 420).
In his research on character education, Lickona (1983, 1991) explained
repeatedly and in detail how these goals may be achieved in the classroom, the home, and the community through a variety of strategies, from
cooperative learning groups and large group discussion to role-playing
and simulation.

Character Education and Contemporary
Research: The Moral System

Two of the major developments in character education in the past thirty years have been the recognition of stage theories of moral development and the functioning of moral thinking as an integral component in the fostering of prosocial moral conduct. Recent research in the social sciences, and especially in child and adolescent development, has built on earlier understandings of moral development and has revealed significant psychological structures in the formation of the human moral system. It refines the moral thinking paradigm of earlier models and, most important for educators, it holds significant promise for mediating much of the controversy surrounding the form and function of character education programs. As Damon (1995) explained:

> In psychological terms, there are at least four overlapping processes that ensure moral awareness from an early age: moral emotions, moral judgment, social cognition, and self-understanding. . . . Each of the processes plays a unique role in disposing young people towards prosocial and away from antisocial engagements. They also work in synchrony, combining with one another in ways that increase one another's effectiveness. The four processes continuously interpenetrate all throughout the course of development, spurring each other's growth. (p. 134)

Social cognition and self-understanding represent no novelty to most classroom teachers because these two concepts form the psychological bedrock of daily instruction. For example, students in English class often examine their own feelings and experiences in relation to a poem, and students in American government class frequently analyze how the Constitution affects their lives every day. Such activities refine how students relate to each other and their world (social cognition) and how they perceive themselves (self-understanding). Moral judgment is also nothing new because in many school districts it has become the philosophical impediment that keeps teachers from actually infusing character education into schooling. This impediment emanates from the lack of consensus on values within the school community, rendering moral judgments increasingly problematic. For instance, a school district that imposes a strict policy against academic cheating and dishonesty may be challenged by parents who claim that some forms of dishonesty (e.g., plagiarism) are actually coping strategies caused by intense academic competition, and thus should be excused or at least handled trivially. Finally, the emotional component of the moral system is often disregarded in character education programs. Yet, ironically, it is this component that holds great promise for enacting such programs in public schools.

Moral emotions or moral sentiments are "feeling states" that contribute to the development of moral values (Damon, 1988, p. 14). Suggesting Piaget's dynamic of assimilation and accommodation (Gallagher & Reid, 1981), Damon (1988) explained that

> children naturally experience many moral feelings in the course of their social engagements. As children reflect on these moral feelings, they question and redefine the values that gave rise to the feelings. Sooner or later the redefined values are tested through conduct, all of which gives rise to new feelings, new reflections, and further redefinitions of the child's moral code. This is the lifeblood of the moral development process. . . . Most scholars believe that moral emotions are a natural component of a child's social repertoire, and that the potential for moral-emotional reactions is present at birth. Some have gone even further in claiming that the moral emotions constitute the one feature of morality that unites humans from all the world's diverse cultures. (p. 13)

Among the more convincing researchers presently examining how moral sentiments undergird the formation of moral thinking and moral conduct is Wilson. In *The Moral Sense* (1993), he has identified at least four of these sentiments: sympathy, fairness, self-control, and duty (p. xiii). While Wilson (1993) and others (Damon, 1995, 1988; Kagan, 1984) contend that these moral feeling states are present at birth and form the basis of later developmental refinements within the moral system, these moral feeling states do not, in themselves, necessarily lead to moral thinking or moral conduct. They are best understood as predispositions to moral conduct. It is the responsibility of caregivers, teachers, and other adults to nurture these moral emotions in children and to guide youth towards thoughtful, socially acceptable conduct. Although they may only be predispositions to moral conduct, the moral sentiments nevertheless can provide a starting point in resolving the debate over the content of character education programs. If these moral feeling states identified by Wilson are present in everyone, even from birth, they could become the general substances of such programs. Sympathy, fairness, self-control, and duty would be nurtured in the classroom through a variety of activities, protocols, and expectations. At the same time, these moral sentiments could be used collectively as the moral compass for making moral judgments. Programs using the moral sentiments and moral judgment jointly would also focus on self-understanding and social cognition, all in an attempt to raise moral awareness, reinforce moral conduct, and provide opportunities for the components of the moral system to interpenetrate each other.

A Lack of Consensus

While it is true that a lack of consensus in many public schools over the shape and purpose of character education is one of the most glaring impediments for undertaking such efforts, powerful cultural forces relating to how we raise our children should also be included among these impediments. In *Greater Expectations: Overcoming the Culture of Indulgence in America's Homes and Schools*, Damon (1995) observed:

> Our heightened concern with children's internal mental states has combined with the increased child-centeredness of modern times to create crippling imbalances in children's views of themselves and the world. When we tell children that their first goal is self-love, we are suggesting to them that they are the center of the universe. By contributing to the already child-centered orientation of modern culture, this emphasis can push a child toward a narcissistic insensitivity to the needs of others. We should not dispute the value of self-love, but we should question its utility as a primary goal in raising and educating children. (p. 77)

Damon's assessment of contemporary childrearing practices should cause us to question the primacy of self-love as the guiding principle within such practices. More importantly, however, his observations are significant because they suggest a positive correlation between excessive child-centeredness and narcissism and between narcissism and social insensitivity. These connections recall Lasch's (1979) equally troubling warning made over twenty years ago in *The Culture of Narcissism: American Life in an Age of Diminishing Expectations*, a warning that links the culture of narcissism to numerous dysfunctions within social institutions, including a multiplicity of failings in schooling. Lasch does not directly examine how cultural narcissism undercuts efforts to engage in character education in the classroom; however, it is possible that the attending self-absorption, feelings of entitlement, grandiosity, and general self-centeredness of the culture of narcissism may compromise efforts by parents and teachers alike to foster the prosocial behavior that is the foundation of character education programs.

Quo Vadis

Character education has, in various forms, been an integral component of education in America since colonial times. It should continue today, not because of historical precedent, but, as Wynne (1985–86) argued, because it is integral to the very process of education. Character education provides opportunities for students to analyze, appreciate, and internalize beliefs, behaviors, and habits of mind that are essential for participating

humanely in democratic societies and for living happy, fulfilled, responsible lives.

Classroom teachers, curriculum specialists, school administrators, community activists, and parents should consider developing character education programs that address all components of the moral system: self-
understanding, social cognition, the moral sense, and moral judgment.
However, they must also address in these programs how the culture of
narcissism may weaken and even subvert components of the moral system.

The Praxis section, chapters 5 through 7, presents approaches and
activities that can be used in specific classroom settings to develop prosocial
behavior that is directly linked to the moral system and that simultaneously
confronts the influences of cultural narcissism. While discussing the specific applications of the moral system, we will emphasize the interactional
aspects of the moral sense and moral judgment, focusing especially on
how Wilson's moral sentiments (duty, self-control, sympathy, and fairness) may be used as standards for evaluating the moral substance of
student behavior. Similarly, in examining how self-understanding and social cognition may be infused into learning activities, we will emphasize
how these two components of the moral system should be kept in balance. Such balance is suggested by Damon (1983) in his analysis of
Baldwin's now-classic explanation of the two-directional structure of social development.

> Children come to know themselves only as a consequence of social interaction of
> many others. . . . An adolescent who learns that he can feel jealous of a rival
> becomes aware that people have the capacity for jealousy. In this manner, the
> child's sense of self and other grows simultaneously, inextricably woven together
> in the course of development. (p. 5)

By stressing the integrated nature of self-understanding and social cognition, we intend to offset any undue or unnecessary preoccupation with
self-understanding which would have the potential for enlarging itself into
narcissistic self-absorption, thereby keeping the student from maximizing
the benefits of social cognition.

The activities in the Praxis chapters will focus on the English language
arts, social studies, mathematics, and science classrooms and will derive
from various learning theories. Close attention will also be given to how
educational technology is especially effective in raising moral awareness
and in revealing the potentially harmful effects of cultural narcissism on
the moral system. The treatment of character education within specific

classroom disciplines will be preceded, first, by a detailed examination of cultural narcissism, second, by a full discussion of the moral system, and third, by an analysis of how educational technology can engender the components of the moral system as well as thwart the influence of cultural narcissism.

Chapter Two

Cultural Narcissism in American Life: Impediments to Character Education

The myth of Narcissus is rich in meaning, generating themes of self-love, self-absorption, and ultimately self-destruction. Sugerman (1976) remarks that Narcissus is "at one and the same time a-social, anti-social, and anti-self. . . . He withdraws his body to a lonely place and his feelings to the loneliness of his own heart. . . . He is the never-to-be-loved lover and from that knowledge he must make the ultimate withdrawal into death" (p. 21).

Despite the psychological nuances of Sugarman's analysis of the Narcissus myth, most Americans probably believe in the narrow denotation that a narcissist is one involved in egoism or egocentrism, or one who displays "love of or sexual desire for one's own body" (*Merriam-Webster's Collegiate Dictionary*, 1998, p. 772). In many ways, these popular understandings of the myth reflect Narcissus' death as captured by Ovid more than two thousand years ago:

> And Narcissus looked long and deep
> Into the clear pool, longing for the Image
> Gazing back at him—pining for its love and
> Embrace, he lunged into the pool, embracing
> The image of himself, drowning in the clear pool.
> Ovid, *The Metamorphosis* (McNiff, 1969, p. 27)

These common understandings of the term are also reflected by Lasch (1979) in *The Culture of Narcissism*; however, Lasch goes beyond these surface-level uses of the term and examines the concept deeply as a psychosocial, cultural phenomenon that pervades much of American life.

Lasch maintains that since the end of World War II, narcissism as a cultural phenomenon and as a pathological syndrome has increased dramatically in the Western industrialized nations, and that in America today it has surfaced as one of the dominant personality types. At first, narcissism as a cultural phenomenon appeared primarily among the upper middle class, but now the phenomenon pervades all socioeconomic levels of contemporary society.

Drawing from the research and clinical experience of Heinz Kohut (1971) and Otto Kernberg (1975), Lasch contends that narcissism can best be understood as a spectrum of personality traits, beliefs, and behaviors. Some of the more pronounced narcissistic traits include an obsession with the present and with being young; a disregard for courtesy, etiquette, and traditional ritual; a need for immediate gratification; a sense of inner emptiness and depression; fear of not being a winner; disturbances in self-esteem; a sense of grandiosity; a need for identifying with celebrity types; an inability to mourn; hypochondria; a need for interminable psychoanalysis; the use of manipulation and deceit to control others; and an inability to make commitments and to engage in sincere, loving relationships (Lasch, 1979).

At one end of the spectrum are those persons, and they include most Americans, who display in their daily lives various patterns of innocuous narcissistic behaviors similar to those listed above; however, the degree is not so pronounced as to limit or weaken social, personal, and professional interaction or compromise a person's ability to engage in stable, loving relationships. At the other end of the scale are those who suffer from pathological narcissism and who exhibit in strident form many if not most of the above listed traits. These persons are socially and personally stilted by self-absorption, they cannot maintain personal commitments, and they are usually unable to engage in sincere loving relationships. In short, their ability to live happy, fulfilled, prosocial lives is seriously impaired (Ryan, 1996).

In examining the etiology of pathological narcissism, Lasch explains how changes within the structure of the modern family contribute to the rise of this more pernicious form of self-absorption (Lasch, 1979). More importantly, he also analyzes how, as cultural phenomena, narcissistic lifeplans and belief systems are encouraged by the media, advertising, business, politics, government, and professional athletics. He argues that even schooling is contributing, although perhaps unwittingly, to the spread of cultural narcissism (Ryan, 1997).

Lasch (1979) presents an account of how school practices during the 1960s and 1970s reflected, as well as abetted, the rise of the narcissistic perspective among school children. For instance, he maintains that decreased student interest in history, foreign languages, and the classics reflects student self-absorption with the present as well as an antipathy toward the past and toward cultures and languages that they consider irrelevant. The rise of electives, he argues, is also a response to student lack of interest in traditional subjects and to the desire of curriculum supervisors to satisfy student clamoring for more relevant material. He indicates, too, that instructional methodologies often play to student demands to be entertained, to be at the center of attention, and to be immediately gratified. This criticism also extends to those techniques for teaching writing that foster creativity and self-expression and that ignore more traditional exercises in rhetoric, which require mastery of principles demanding self-discipline and structure. He concludes that the overall slippage of academic achievement throughout American education since the 1960s derives largely from lack of self-discipline, from self-absorption, from a sense of entitlement, and from self-gratification, all part of the culture of narcissism (Lasch, 1979).

While Lasch's indictment of schooling appears to underscore those practices found mostly in the middle and upper grades, Katz (1993) has more recently examined how narcissism, in the guise of self-esteem, has also infiltrated preschool, kindergarten, and elementary school. In "All about me: Are we developing our children's self-esteem or their narcissism?" Katz, anticipating Damon's (1995) similar observations, warned that "as commendable as it is for children to have high self-esteem, many of the practices advocated in pursuit of this goal may instead inadvertently develop narcissism in the form of excessive preoccupation with oneself" (p. 20). Katz's observations reinforce Lasch's general thesis regarding the pervasiveness of narcissism in American life, as well as the potential to abet narcissistic traits among young children and adolescents. (Ryan, 1997).

Although Lasch's thesis is a large theoretical brushstroke that is appealing in its logic and is replete with illustrations from contemporary culture, his thesis is not without shortcomings. His assessment of the prevalence of pathological narcissism, as opposed to cultural narcissism, throughout American society was at best overstated (Ryan, 1985). And in his discussion of schooling, he totally disregarded the appearance of normal adolescent egocentrism. Despite these omissions, he was correct in noting that narcissism, as a cultural phenomenon, has permeated almost all phases of American life. With its focus on self-absorption and self-aggrandizement and with its general disregard for others, it is not surprising that cultural narcissism has become a serious obstacle for teachers trying to emphasize in their classrooms the prosocial behavior that is the cornerstone of character education (Ryan, 1997). More to the point, narcissism is an equally potent force in fracturing the components of the moral system that should be the foundations of character education programs.

A Reciprocal Dynamic

Damon (1995) may be correct in claiming that the components of the moral system—self-understanding, social cognition, moral sentiments, moral judgment—actually provide redundancy to the moral system. As he explained it: "Where one process fails, another intercedes to ensure the moral act" (Damon, 1995, p. 134). However, the potency and ubiquity of cultural narcissism can pollute all of these components, rendering the redundancy of the components seriously compromised.

The process of developing self-understanding and social cognition is a reciprocal dynamic, with growth in one area influencing growth in the other. As Shaffer (1994) observed, social cognition is "how children come to understand the thoughts, intentions, emotions, and behaviors of themselves and other people; how they conceptualize their social relationships with parents, peers, friends, and authority figures (for example teachers); and how this knowledge influences their social behavior and personality development" (p. 106). Similarly, self-understanding or self-concept develops during early childhood and continues throughout one's lifetime. However, during adolescence there is a focused concern with a major developmental task: "the need to establish a firm, future-oriented self-portrait, or identity, with which to approach the responsibilities of young adulthood" (Shaffer, 1994, p. 210). Damon (1983) noted that "the individual's sense of identity guides the individual cognitively, affectively, and behaviorally through all of life's choices that have some bearing upon what one is like. As such, identity must be composed of specifics" (p. 325). If identity is composed of specifics, adolescents who have internalized the particular proselytizings of cultural narcissism, from rock songs, magazine ads, afternoon soap operas, sitcoms, films, videos, and even schooling, will have begun to process into their identities these specifics, which necessarily will impact upon their social cognition as well. Thus, such adolescents might predictably display feelings of grandiosity and entitlement, a general sense of self-absorption, and a need for immediate gratification (all part of their self-understanding) as well as exhibit a disregard for courtesy and etiquette, a devaluation of others, the use of manipulation and deceit to control others, and the inability to make commitments (all elements of their social cognition).

Just as the forces of cultural narcissism can subvert the development of social cognition and self-understanding towards prosocial endeavors, these same forces can likewise affect the moral sentiments and moral judgment. In reflecting on the increase of antisocial behavior among so many of our youth, Damon (1995) also explained how everyone is predisposed by the moral sentiments to behave morally and how cultural forces can taint the cultivation of the these sentiments:

> Every infant enters the world prepared to respond socially, and in a moral manner, to others. Every child has the capacity to acquire moral character. The necessary emotional response systems, budding cognitive awareness, and personal dispositions are there from the start. Although, unfortunately, every child does not grow into a responsible and caring person, the potential to do so is native to every member of the species. This is just one of many reasons why it is such a tragic waste when a young person drifts into a condition of moral apathy— or worse, into a frenzy of antisocial behavior. When an entire generation shows signs of moving in such directions, one must look for the cultural forces that are leading them astray. Natural dispositions (i.e. moral sentiments), however robust, are not in themselves enough to ensure moral character. In forming a person's mature moral sense, culture and nature work together from the time of birth, in multiple ways. . . . (p. 132)

Damon (1995) did not mention narcissism among the cultural forces that are leading so many of our youth towards antisocial behavior. Nevertheless, if American culture is as saturated with narcissistic belief systems and self-lifeplans to the degree that Lasch maintained, then the cultivation and refinement of the moral sentiments, especially those identified by Wilson (1993)—fairness, duty, self-control, sympathy—would be understandably hampered by counterurgings for immediate gratification, manipulation of others, self-absorption, and self-aggrandizement.

Moral judgment "refers to one's manner of determining prescriptive choices about social conduct and one's means of evaluating matters of justice, care, truthfulness, responsibility, and ethical duty" (Damon, 1995, p. 133). Here again, a person whose self-concept and social cognition have been sufficiently imbued with the precepts of cultural narcissism would most probably have considerable difficulty selecting "prescriptive choices about social conduct" and evaluating related ethical matters in ways that would benefit others, rather than the self.

Seeds of Narcissism

Lasch's argument that the culture of narcissism has indeed infiltrated many quarters of American life is compelling. Yet, it is important to keep in mind that not everyone processes these narcissistic messages the same way nor to the same degree, and not all manifestations of narcissistic behavior are necessarily pathological. However, some persons do develop narcissistic personality disorders which, theoretically at least, might require clinical treatment. These disorders occur primarily because one of the tasks of rapprochement, the deflation of infantile grandiosity and omnipotence, is never fully realized (Masterman, 1981). The rapprochement period of development (about 18 months through four years of age) is when a child experiences separation and individuation from its caregiver, usually the mother. For a healthy self-concept to develop, it is critical for the child to recognize some disappointment in its mother, recognition that forces the child to develop a sense of identity that gradually becomes separate from the mother. But these episodes of disappointment must be balanced by maternal warmth, support, and understanding that addresses the child's needs and overall temperament.

> As the child begins to perceive his mother's limitations and fallibility, he relinquishes the image of maternal perfection and begins to take over many of her functions—to provide for his own care and comfort. An idealized image of the mother lives on in the child's unconscious thoughts. Diminished, however, by the daily experiences of maternal fallibility, it comes to be associated not with fantasies of infantile omnipotence but with the ego's modest, growing mastery of its environment. Disappointment with the mother, brought about not only by the child's perception that he does not occupy the exclusive place in her affections, makes it possible for the child to relinquish her undivided love while internalizing the image of maternal love . . . and incorporating her life-giving functions. (Lasch, 1979, pp. 294–295)

Relating this process to contemporary culture, Lasch explained that the culture of narcissism has influenced the family in such ways that many mothers, in being influenced by narcissistic self-lifeplans and belief systems, are increasingly interfering with their children's normal separation process. "By treating the child as an 'exclusive possession,' she encourages an exaggerated sense of his own importance; at the same time she makes it difficult for him to acknowledge his disappointment in her shortcomings" (Lasch, 1979, p. 294). In short, this pathological form of narcissism arises during rapprochement as a result of "chronically cold, unsympathetic parents who fail to provide the infant the love and attention necessary for psychological health" (Berman, 1990, p. 24).

It should be noted that while the roots of narcissistic personality disorders can be traced to the rapprochement phase of development (Kernberg, 1975; Masterman, 1981; Rothstein, 1980), the child-rearing inconsistencies described by Lasch and others do not in themselves necessarily cause such disorders. Other variables can intervene, including the child's temperament, the consistency and duration of the disappointment, and the child's relationship to her parents before and after the disappointment (Rothstein, 1980). While it is correct that the type and degree of the disappointment, as well as other variables identified by Rothstein, may indeed mollify and in some cases even prevent a narcissistic personality disorder, it is nonetheless true that the prevalence and seductiveness of narcissistic self-lifeplans certainly have the potential for creating disturbances in family dynamics that can influence a child's rapprochement, thus possibly leading to pathology. In this context, it should not come as a surprise that psychotherapists have noted an increase in the number of narcissistic personality disorders since the 1950s (Sennett, 1974), the same time period that Lasch identifies as the beginnings of the culture of narcissism in American life.

Narcissism in Present-Day American Life and Education

An astute observer of contemporary American life will notice that the culture of narcissism, as described by Lasch more than twenty-five years ago, shows no signs of waning as we move into the twenty-first century. It continues to influence various quarters of both popular and refined culture, and it is found increasingly in electronic media, where narcissistic belief systems and self-lifeplans are transmitted every day into our homes via radios, TVs, and computers.

Television commercials continue to promise immediate gratification and even self-fulfillment if we would only purchase the prescribed clothing, soft drink, toothpaste, or car. While adolescents are frequently the targets of such marketing, many shows, such as *Beverly Hills 90210* and *Real World*, are intentionally written to exploit not so much teenage consumerism as to reflect the crisis of adolescent identity formation. Countless young people religiously block out time in their personal schedules to watch these shows, which many find entertaining and personally relevant. But a close analysis of many of the characters in these minidramas reveals personalities whose identity search has degenerated into insensitive self-absorption, resulting in flights of grandiosity, entitlement, and devaluation of others. Considering that adolescents are especially influenced by what they watch on TV (Van Hoose, 1980), such depictions are at the very least disquieting in terms of their potential for proseltyzing these components of cultural narcissism.

Adolescents, as well as adults, are also exposed to narcissistic self-lifeplans and belief systems in a host of sitcom characters from *Friends* to *Frasier.* No sitcom, however, more succinctly captures the contemporary culture of narcissism than *Seinfeld*. Media critic Heller (1998) noted that the show "was always, in just about *every* episode, about consummate self-centeredness . . ." (p. F1). Moreover, psychologist Rosen Spector (cited in Weiner, 1998), commenting on the Kramer character, was struck by his "perverse grandiosity, his lack of empathy for other people, his sense of entitlement" (p. F10). These citations illustrate elements of narcissism as described by Lasch, as do many talk shows on TV and radio which focus on narcissistic exhibitionism. Here guests unabashedly expose the intimacies of their private lives to audiences that revel in uncovering more and more details. Recently, the Internet, too, has become the site of various exhibitionistic displays, which range from live human births to personal web sites where 24-hour video cameras capture intimate details of women's personal lives. Even Hollywood has contributed to this exhibitionism, although satirically, in Ron Howard's *EDtv* (1999) whose plot focuses on following the character Ed around with a video camera and filming his most intimate conversations and personal activities. Increasing numbers of explicit, sexually oriented web sites also reflect Lasch's analysis of narcissistic promiscuity that pervades contemporary culture, as do the numbers of cable movies that contain gratuitous, sexually explicit scenes.

On an equally disturbing note, syndicated columnist Pitts (1998) attributed so much of adolescent violence to "our national culture of brattiness" (p. A112). Pitts (1998) claimed that such children are spoiled because

> they live lives of entitlement, their everyday waking thoughts revolve around themselves. . . . We blame so many dysfunctions on low self-esteem, but I wonder if some don't suffer from the opposite affliction—if some aren't so steeped in self-esteem that they can't see or sympathize beyond the borders of their own lives. (p. A12)

These observations from the popular press encapsulate the highpoints of Bushman and Baumeister's (1998) research, which examined relationships between violence and narcissism. They pointed out that recently "American society has come to look upon self-esteem as an unmitigated good and a cure for a variety of personal and social problems. . . . Consistent with this view, it has been widely asserted that low self-esteem is the cause of violence" (p. 219). Their research challenged these assumptions and demonstrated that "inflated, grandiose, or unjustified favorable views of the self would be most prone to causing aggression" (p. 221). They maintained that narcissism is marked by a sense of superiority over others. Even though they themselves are not directly threatened, narcissists often intimidate or attack others because of their need to maintain their feelings of superiority (Bushman & Baumeister, 1998). In the context of this research, classroom instruction and activities which emphasize the importance and cultivation of the self, and which are not correlated to achievement, for example, those described previously by Katz (1993), become doubly ominous. Not only do such activities have the potential of fostering narcissistic grandiosity, entitlement, and overall self-absorption, but they also heighten the index for aggression.

Ironically, many classroom activities and methods of instruction that have the potential for generating features of the culture of narcissism are also essential components of effective teaching. For instance, teachers should help students personalize the curriculum by providing opportunities for students to see connections to their personal lives. As Kindsvatter, Wilen, and Ishler (1992) explained, teachers can personalize learning "by relating the concept to the students' current knowledge and experience. Once this has been accomplished, the new content, which is an extension of the abstraction, is presented with a higher probability of being understood by the students" (p. 91). Attempts at personalizing content are essential for expanding student interest, for enhancing meaning, and for addressing different learning styles. But a constant emphasis on such techniques can exacerbate the cultural narcissism that pervades much of the adolescent worldview. In short, such personalizations must be ultimately redirected to the content as a way of enhancing understanding; otherwise, the personalizations can turn upon themselves, resulting in self-aggrandizement and self-absorption but falling short of improving content mastery (Ryan, 1996).

Pedagogical emphasis on personalization was common during the 1970s, when students were often encouraged to generate "me-centered" questions that were frequently far afield of the content (Sommers, 1984, p. 383). For example, when students were introduced to the moral origins of the Bill of Rights, they were often asked to consider the following: "What rights do you have in your family?" "When was the last time you signed a petition?" No doubt students would find these questions engaging, but unless redirected thoughtfully to the purpose of the lesson, the questions alone would contribute little to understanding the moral origins of the Bill of Rights, an activity that requires a historical and a philosophical context that students intuitively cannot provide. Sykes (1995) observed that these "me-centered" questions also permeate many classrooms today. For instance, he cited the following that were used to personalize material on the Civil War: "Why didn't Sherman and Stonewall Jackson feel good about each other?" "Compare the disputes of the Union and the Confederacy to the last time Brenda and Tiffany couldn't agree on when to go to the mall" (p. 4).

While "me-centered" questions have appeared with increasing regularity in social studies classrooms, such questions have markedly proliferated in English language arts classes where reader-response practices dominate (Beach & Marshall, 1991; Tompkins, 1980). Here, students are not encouraged to examine literary texts for an author's meaning or for a deeper understanding of how the literature reflects the culture that contributed to its production. Instead, students are led to analyze the literature solely in the context of their own experiences, without attention to a possible shared interpretation posited in the text itself. In many ways, reader-response practices are a needed antidote for strict textual analysis that in many classrooms have become excessively routinized, resulting in dullness and boredom rather than in literary understanding, appreciation, and stimulation. Reader-response pedagogy can indeed be motivational and invigorating. But unless it is balanced with other perspective-taking activities that lead students out of themselves and their own experiences, reader-response pedagogy has the potential for amplifying in students the cultural narcissism that already pervades so many classrooms throughout the country.

Since the 1980s, the teaching of writing has also been transformed to include a repositioning of the self at the center of various assignments, whether creative or expository. Such assignments are effective in plumbing the nature, strengths, and weaknesses of the self, and this is especially true during adolescence. Yet these writing activities should ultimately help reconnect the student to the outward world of society at large. Recognizing the need to balance the innerworld with the outerworld, Wright (1980) observed:

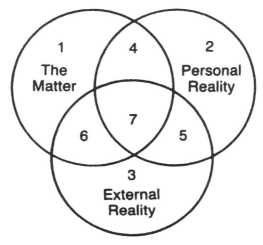

Figure 2.1 Question Circle System. Permission to use granted by the National Council Teachers of English

Writing not only contributes to the development of the self but contributes to the development of the values of a community and a culture. Discovering the self, therefore, is natural and essential. Writing plays an important role in our Age of Narcissism. We move inward in order to make sense of the world (p. 28).

Teachers should be sensitive to how these personal realities can for many students be the endpoint of learning, and how the external reality of the academic content may be obscured by the affective appeal to the self. Teachers should therefore consider using Kindsvatter, Wilen, and Ishler's (1996) Questioning Circle as a balance to the self-absorption implicit in these personalizations. The Questioning-Circle System engages students in a series of questions that blend the content, the personal reality, and the external reality.

1. The matter: What are the causes of acid rain?
2. Personal reality: Have you personally seen acid[-]rain damage and, if so, how would you describe your experience?
3. External reality: How has the acid-rain problem influenced the politics of other countries?
4. The matter/personal reality: How might you personally be affected by the acid-rain problem?
5. Personal reality/external reality: What could you do to bring the issues and problems associated with acid rain to the attention of other people?

6. The matter/external reality: What are the issues affecting the relationship between Canada and the United States related to the acid-rain problem?
7. The matter/personal reality/external reality: Why should we as citizens of a global society care about acid rain?

The "Questioning Circle System" has the advantage of appealing to students' personal realities (which enhances interest and motivation), while leading the students out of their own worlds (which fosters perspective-taking and social cognition) and maximizing content mastery.

One of the most popular approaches to teaching and learning today is constructivism, an approach that, when used exclusively in the classroom, has the potential for fostering self-absorption and grandiosity. Kindsvatter et al. (1996) explained that constructivism is not so much a method or a strategy as it is a theory about knowledge and learning. "Teachers are to help students relate new content to the knowledge they already know, as well as to have them process and apply the new knowledge" (p. 112).

Countless articles and textbooks endorse constructivist activities which many contend are highly motivational because it places the student's experience at the center of learning. Critics, however, argue that constructivists not only overemphasize and misunderstand the role of experience in learning, but they also believe that

> there is no firm or fixed reality, no stable or fixed truths that can be objectively presented or understood. . . . Every single individual can construct his own meanings, each different from the others. Reality . . . is not the same from person to person. It is merely subjective and relative, and truth is ultimately unknowable. (Sykes, 1995, p. 135).

Damon (1995), while less philosophical than Sykes, attested to constructivist influences in the classroom. Damon pointed out that constructivism is widely used in the lower grades and that such practice often degenerates into "a grab bag of loosely structured storytelling, singing, untutored arts and crafts, play activities, and frequent partying" (p. 104). Citing what he calls "the constructivist fallacy," Damon also argued that constructivists overlooked the "interactional roots of all intellectual achievement." As he explained the learning process:

> Virtually all serious theoretical work in child development now assumes that learning is neither a solipsistic expression nor a passive experience for the child but rather that it results from complex, extended, and multifaceted engagements between learners, teachers, and the rest of the real world. . . . Simply put, children can-

not learn wholly on their own: for intellectual growth, they need to be instructed, prodded, challenged, corrected, and assisted by people who are trying to teach them something. . . . Learning is more than a matter of realizing one's incipient inner intimations. Above all, it requires an external structure of reality, of information, of communication, and of social supports. Above all, it requires an organized presentation of a systematic body of knowledge. (pp. 104–105)

Damon (1995) is correct in emphasizing the interactional dimension of learning, especially the role of the teacher in helping students make sense of classroom experiences and activities. In this way, teachers can guard students from slipping too deeply into the subjectivity, relativity, and self-absorption that can result from constructivistic classroom experiences where an exclusive emphasis on personal meaning can breed narcissistic habits of mind and grandiose self-concepts. In short, self-focused, constructivist approaches can be effective instructional tools provided that they are balanced with social, interactional strategies that include the development of not just self-understanding but also social cognition, the moral sense, and moral judgment.

Positive Narcissism

As noted earlier, the term *narcissistic*, like the terms *egotistical* and *self-centeredness*, is understood by most people in a very narrow denotative sense, and all three terms usually conjure up negative feelings and reactions towards those people who are so described. Yet, many of us probably know people who display many of the traits identified by Lasch as part of the culture of narcissism. They may be self-absorbed: at times they manifest feelings of entitlement and grandiosity; they may even engage in consistent devaluation of others. But these same people frequently engage in very prosocial behavior. They are often the first to lend us money and to assist us with a difficult chore. On a more global scale, they frequently participate in social projects designed to rebuild communities after natural disasters. These prosocial behaviors may at first glance seem to contradict the profiles described by Lasch of those who have been markedly influenced by the culture of narcissism. But Lasch has completely overlooked such people, those described by psychologists as positive narcissists (Rothstein, 1980; Kohut, 1971). These people share many of the narcissistic characteristics identified by Lasch, but their narcissism is clearly not pathological. Not only can they engage in meaningful personal relationships, but such people are often at the forefront of positive social change and even philanthropy. Commenting on this positive variety of narcissism, Goldberg (1980) observed that narcissism should not be viewed as a negative construct but rather as the source of humankind's ingenuity, creativity, and exploration. "Narcissism, in its positive sense, is the unwillingness to be dissuaded, discouraged, or ridiculed against giving birth to the most audacious and grandiose projects. It is commitment to passion as the enrichment of human experience" (p. 12).

Goldberg's assessment of the positive dimensions of narcissism reminds us that these attitudes and behaviors need not be destructive if the narcissistic energy is directed outward towards prosocial good. When discussing and confronting cultural narcissism, teachers should therefore highlight these distinctions between positive and negative narcissism. And they should also discuss the moral system in the context of these distinctions. For instance, a social studies teacher might want to emphasize how positive narcissism may have motivated such persons as Susan B. Anthony, Frederick Douglass, Thomas Paine, Elizabeth Cady Stanton, and Harriet Tubman. Teachers would stress that the passion of these figures for rebelling against the social order was grounded ultimately in a sense of duty to advance human equality, and how that passion led them to challenge the social policies of those times that militated against fairness and justice. Such classroom discussion would not only present and clarify the concept of positive narcissism, but it would also emphasize how the moral sentiments, in these cases duty and fairness, relate to moral judgment and moral action (Ryan, 1997).

In summary, we agree that Lasch (1979) and more recently Damon (1995) are accurate in their explanations of how social institutions and child-rearing practices have spawned increases in narcissistic personality traits among many of our youth today. We are not endorsing Lasch's view that such manifestations are increasingly pathological, nor do we see his claims of pathology in any way relevant to our contention that cultural narcissism is interfering with character education in the schools. On this point, we believe that American school teachers will agree that many of the characteristics of cultural narcissism described by Lasch (feelings of entitlement, perfection and grandiosity, devaluation of others; a disregard for courtesy, etiquette, and traditional ritual; a need for immediate gratification; self-absorption; the use of deceit and manipulation to control others; and the inability to make commitments) have been internalized by many school-aged children. Where the degree of internalization among many students has been dramatic, we contend that infusing prosocial behavior into the classroom will be problematic. We therefore argue that teachers who intend to infuse character education into the classroom through cultivating all elements of the moral system will first need to sensitize their students to the influence of the culture of narcissism, focusing on how it can compromise prosocial behavior and how it can, in some cases, ironically advance the social good.

Chapter Three

The Moral System and Cultural Narcissism

The components of the moral system (Damon, 1995), consisting of self-understanding, social cognition, moral judgment, and moral emotions or sentiments, "work in synchrony, combining with one another in ways that increase one another's effectiveness. The four processes continuously interpenetrate all throughout the course of development, spurring each other's growth" (pp. 133–134). While these processes may foster each other's development, a person's overall moral system is likewise grounded in a particular culture. And where the culture directly or indirectly emphasizes the benefits of narcissistic belief systems and self-lifeplans, the development of the moral system would necessarily be compromised in ways that would consistently position the self over the other, the individual over the community. Where a person's moral system is heavily laden with many of the elements of narcissism described by Lasch (1979) in Chapter 2, moral conduct, which frequently requires self-control and even self-denial, would also be compromised.

This chapter will examine the components of the moral system, focusing especially on the interpenetration of the parts. It will also explain how cultural narcissism may, in various ways, pollute the development of the moral system particularly during mid- and later childhood as well as during adolescence, thereby causing considerable challenges for teachers engaged in character education.

Self-Understanding and Social Cognition

Understanding the self and understanding others is a reciprocal dynamic, with self-understanding leading to a fuller appreciation of others, and with deeper understanding of others leading to insight into the self. The richness of this dynamic was captured by Baldwin (1902) in his classic analysis of social development:

> The growing child is able to think of self in varying terms as varying situations impress themselves upon him. . . . The development of the child's personality could not go on at all without the constant modification of his sense of himself by suggestions from others. So he himself, at every stage, is really in part someone else, even in his own thought of himself. (p. 23)

As the self is constructed by data received from others, knowledge of others is constructed from data coming in from the opposite direction. For instance, a young child who understands that she becomes upset when she is treated unjustly will assume that other people will also react this way in similar situations. And a teenage football player who becomes jealous of a rival player may learn that all people have a tendency to experience jealousy in similar contexts. Hence, a child's self-understanding and understanding of others grow simultaneously, and they influence each other throughout the person's lifetime (Damon, 1983).

Research suggests that the capacity for participating in this reciprocal dynamic is present at birth, "with newborns coming into the world equipped with certain predispositions enabling them to engage in early social exchanges, provided that they are part of a responsive caregiving system" (Sroufe, Cooper, & DeHart, 1996, p. 201). As infants grow and the universe of human contact expands, they are provided countless opportunities to learn about themselves and others. During the second through sixth year, the child develops an especially refined conceptualization of the self as an object (Kagan, 1994). For instance, Lewis and Brooks-Gunn (1979) tested children's self-knowledge by analyzing their abilities to recognize themselves in pictures, mirrors, and on television. The researchers found that two-year-olds could recognize pictures of themselves, and when seeing themselves reflected in mirrors, the children would touch their noses to remove a spot of rouge placed there, indicating that they recognized the reflection in the mirror as their own. Even with language acquisition there is the suggestion that the self as object is highlighted in all events (Kagan, 1994). This, for instance, is reflected in the child's use of self-pronouns such as *I*, *me*, and *mine*. Because the child is more likely to describe her own activities rather than similar activities of others, it is inferred that the child is preoccupied with her own actions. By age two, there is evidence that the child is aware of her ability to act, to influence others, and to meet her own standards, all of which indicate that the child's self-understanding and social cognition are developing.

During middle childhood, opportunities for peer interaction increase dramatically, providing for deeper understanding of the self and of others. One of the most influential phenomenona that enhances this two-dimensional understanding is social play. Examining groups of three through five-year-olds at play, Garvey (as cited in Damon, 1983) observed that play enhances children's turn-taking capabilities and fosters the joint development of social play-themes. For example, youngsters may have a limited number of play props (e.g., big-wheels, cars, dolls, etc.) and thus may be forced to share these props in rhythmic turn-taking. Similarly, in channeling the direction of the play-themes, children may modify traditional roles being imitated (e.g., the role of a mother, father, firefighter, doctor, etc.) to meet the requirements of the play script. Once more, play script redirection provides contexts for shared turn taking among children who imaginatively control the movement of the play.

In refining social perspective-taking skills, play can enhance the child's overall socialization (Mead, 1934). This is especially important to their broader social development because at about the age of two, children have an understanding of the "possession rule" (Kagan, 1994; Sroufe et al., 1996). Hence, in sharing toys, children must overcome their feelings of ownership of objects so that they may be shared, which provides social scaffolding for later sharing and turn taking. Moreover, the symbolic nature of play can provide a context for the child's emotional life to be enriched through a variety of expressions not available in everyday, reality-bound living (Damon, 1983). In this sense, Vygotsky calls play the child's *zone of proximal development* because play generates the conditions for the child's acquisition of new imaginative and social competencies (Damon, 1983).

The development of social play during the first six years of childhood has strong implications for self-understanding and for knowledge of others. Such play also connects to the moral sentiments and moral judgment, the other components of the moral system. As Vygotsky suggested (1976), play provides the child opportunities to act on the moral feeling states that may arise as part of the play-theme, for example, the empathy, sympathy, and responsibility arising from a play script calling for the care of a sick baby doll. These feelings of social responsibility and their attending action also relate to the child's moral judgment, for the child's (i.e., the child-as-parent's) obligation to care for the sick doll as being the right thing to do at that time in the play script. Yet, play may also provide another context for cultural narcissism to surface and/or for a child's pathological narcissism to be nurtured and amplified. Chapter 2 explained the etiology of pathological narcissism as a phenomenon that, through a combination of the child's temperament and the parent's child-rearing practices, gestates at about the same years that play becomes part of the child's social repertoire. In the case of pathological narcissism, the child's sense of entitlement and grandiosity would influence the child's turn-taking abilities and script-sharing responsibilities. In such instances, a child might hoard her toys and dictate that the play-theme unfold according to her demands. Even where the child's narcissism is cultural and not pathological, the same type of resistance to social turn-taking and overall cooperation within play activities can result. Left unchecked, the culturally narcissistic child may grow in her feelings of entitlement, grandiosity, and self-absorption, and may reject within the play script the imposition of rules and standards of behavior, which are integral features of moral judgment. Commenting upon such a child in the abstract, Coles (1997) remarked that such a person has never been taught impulse control and the need to delay gratification. Because of these shortcomings the child has "[taken] a giant step towards self-importance, egoism, grandiosity, the swagger of someone not just plentifully given to but on whom the world has doted ceaselessly, so that rules and frustration tolerance have had no chance to develop" (p. 87).

One of the hallmarks of play behavior is the child's development of the concept of a friend and a recognition that other people, including peers, have rights and intentions (Smetana, 1989). It would be difficult, however, for the narcissistic child described by Coles to recognize the rights of peers to engage in any play activity that would not enhance the narcissistic child's self-concept. Furthermore, like the adult narcissist who can neither make commitments nor maintain sincere relationships (Lasch, 1979), the narcissistic child would have difficulty maintaining friendships and honoring commitments. Finally, Coles's narcissist exhibits no capacity for delaying immediate gratification or rule following. These shortcomings would compromise social growth in the arena of play, and they would also offer dramatic challenges for elementary school teachers who may confront the narcissistic child in character education programs, particularly where such programs emphasized self-control, duty, and responsibility.

Once in elementary school, the child's world expands considerably and, depending on the school, this transition might place the child with others from various ethnic, racial, religious, and socioeconomic backgrounds. For perhaps the first time, the enlargement of the peer group, as well as the diverse mix of personalities within the group, provides the child a much larger baseline against which to compare and contrast her physical, cognitive, and social skills. Preschoolers have the ability to compare and contrast themselves to others, but they generally do so in terms of physical traits and physical activities. For instance, a five-year old might say, "I am different from Selina because I have brown hair," or "I like to play baseball in the schoolyard," or "I go to nursery school" (Sroufe et al., 1996). In middle childhood, however, these comparative-contrastive insights develop beyond the physical to include inner thoughts, feelings, abilities, and attributes (Selman, 1980).

In the elementary school classroom, children are now able to measure their own achievements, strengths, shortcomings, and weaknesses in relation to other children. These self-social measurements relate to Erikson's (1963) industry vs. inferiority crisis, a psychosocial period of development that unfolds during the elementary school years. At this time, the child struggles with mastering the tool world of literacy and technology as she prepares for later schooling and/or the world of work. In the classroom, she is encouraged to master reading, arithmetic, social studies, and science, while also being introduced to a work ethic that emphasizes completion of homework and projects and includes working alone and with others. A sense of industry will result when the child accomplishes these tasks. "If not, a sense of inferiority may arise, discouraging further attempts to produce and excel" (Damon, 1983, p. 224).

Through self-social measurements, a child may find that he excels in geography, arithmetic, and football, but is not so strong in reading or in doing show-and-tell in front of his classmates. These shortcomings would not necessarily lead to a complete sense of inferiority because they are balanced with accomplishments in other areas. More to the point, these insights enhance self-understanding and social cognition. They result from large-group instruction and teacher-pupil interaction, but such insights are especially pronounced in small, cooperative learning groups where children have greater opportunities to make up-close comparisons and contrasts with each other. For the child-narcissist, however, these comparisons can lead to frustration if other children in the class or the group are perceived by the narcissist as more academically, athletically, or socially successful. Because the narcissistic child has not developed frustration tolerance (Coles, 1997), such frustration can lead to various forms of acting-out behavior which disrupts the class but which also thrusts the child to center stage, thereby inflating his egoism and sense of grandiosity.

Some acting-out behavior may be more passive-aggressive in nature, a feature also used by the narcissistic child as a defense against affronts to her inflated ego. For instance, while it is true that self-understanding and social cognition is a reciprocal dynamic (Baldwin, 1902), the self is none-theless one's own personal construction. While other children may pro-vide feedback that the narcissistic child may choose to incorporate into the self, the child is the sole arbiter of how to interpret this feedback. As Damon (1983) explained this process in a larger context, "the person has the power not only to decide upon the defining characteristics of self, but also to choose which categories of characteristics (physical, psychologi-cal, and so on) are to be considered and how they are to be ordered" (p. 233). In expanding these points further, Mitchell (1992) noted that nar-cissists ignore and/or distort realities that challenge their own grandiosity and felt quality of perfection:

> Narcissists bend information to fit their desires. This bending does not occur in all areas, but it consistently occurs whenever emotional needs are at issue. The narcissist's understanding of why people behave as they do is contaminated by projection and denial. Frequently they simply ignore what doesn't fit. . . . [This ability to bend reality is] the intellectual style of all narcissists regardless of age, intellectual power, or social skill because their style of thought requires them to ignore data which takes them out of their own fascination with themselves. (p. 72)

Thus, the narcissistic child, who in a math activity confronts a peer with superior aptitude for converting fractions to decimals, may take out a book, claiming that reading (for which she has great talent) is more important and more interesting than mathematics, or perhaps she may take out her speller and simply ignore her rival altogether. In either case, her passive-aggressive reaction would reinforce her self-insight that she was superior to her rival and, couched in Erikson's (1963) assessment of elementary school activity, that she was industrious and by no means inferior.

It should also be pointed out that by about third grade, children are capable of conscious deception, and they can manipulate the relation between internal and external reality (Selman, 1980). Whereas very young children do not seem to distinguish between a person's inner psychologi-cal experiences and their external words or actions, children by age 8 or 9 "recognize that what people say and do need not conform to what they may think and feel" (Sroufe et al., 1996, p. 457). These insights allow the child-narcissist not only to claim that mathematics is not important, but it may also prompt the child to practice various forms of deceit and manipu-lation on her peers to achieve her own goals, inflate her ego, and main-tain her sense of entitlement. Here, she may misrepresent and/or magnify her rival's weaknesses in other academic subjects (e.g., reading, geography) and broadcast these to the class, or she may lure others in joining her in off-task reading, especially when the reading may include higher grade level (e.g., weekly news magazines or secondary school novels) or contraband materials (e.g., comic books). On a cruder level, she may even ridicule her rival's clothing and/or her physical appearance, all in an attempt to inflate her own ego and devalue her rival's accomplishments. Mitchell (1992) captured these response behaviors in his summary of Fromm's observations: "The narcissist's perceptions of reality are such that everything belonging to the self is highly valued [and] . . . everything belonging to another person is devalued, minimized or ridiculed. One's clothing, physique, intellect, method of getting to school, everything is superior to others" (p. 68).

As the above examples suggest, a narcissistic child would pose numerous challenges for the classroom teacher, and these challenges may be exacerbated by further attempts at doing character education. An elementary teacher following Lickona's (1988) recommendations may combat egocentrism and individualism, may foster moral awareness, and may construct a moral community based upon fairness, caring, and participation. If the narcissistic child could not tolerate the ego challenges and frustrations inherent in small group academic instruction, then these character education goals, structured explicitly to foster community, cooperation, and sharing, and designed to confront one's egocentrism, could become explosive in the classroom. Nonetheless, elementary teachers must foster these goals, while also understanding how cultural narcissism can render the development of such prosocial behavior and moral conduct increasingly difficult. And while manifestations of cultural narcissism become more evident in the upper elementary and middle school grades, these appearances become even more pervasive and apparent in the secondary classroom where the emotional *sturm* and *drang* of adolescence thrusts the struggle for self-understanding at the center of almost all social interaction.

Two of the most significant developments in adolescence which have direct implication for self-understanding and social cognition are the rise of formal operational thinking and the pursuit of a consolidated personality, each of which nourishes the other as each unfolds. Although these two developments are dynamically integrated, the complexity of each is better understood when analyzed separately. Thus, formal operations will be discussed first, followed by an examination of consolidated personality.

Developing Formal Operational Thinking

Formal operational reasoning includes "the ability to think hypothetically, to imagine a range of possibilities and future events, and to think systematically about one's own thinking" (Damon, 1983, p. 309). Applying these to specific learning contexts, Elkind (1984) added that formal operational thinking helps "young people to go beyond the here and now, to grasp historical time and celestial space, to comprehend abstract subjects like philosophy, algebra, and calculus, and to appreciate simile, metaphor, and parody" (p. 25). Formal operational thinking also permits the teenager to plumb the depths of her own thinking which also leads to heightened degrees of self-consciousness and self-centeredness. Hughes and Noppe (1991) pointed out that according to Piaget, egocentrism, in some form, is part of all stages of intellectual development and that the adolescent formal operational thinker is not exempt from such self-centeredness. In the social context, this self-centeredness is marked by a failure to distinguish one's own thought processes from those of other persons. This explains why so many adolescents feel that if something is important in their own universe, everyone must perceive this event or fact with equal attention and seriousness. For instance, when younger teenagers go with their parents to the shopping mall, they frequently walk behind or in front of their parents, believing that other teenagers are looking at them and will later make fun of them. Similarly, a teenager may refuse to go to the corner mailbox to mail a letter because she does not want to be seen in public wearing out-of-style sneakers. These examples of heightened self-consciousness reveal what Elkind (1984, p. 33) referred to as the *imaginary audience*. Here, teenagers perceive themselves as being on stage and that *everyone* is as much concerned about and aware of their physical appearance as they are.

According to Mitchell (1992), these heightened degrees of self-consciousness, self-centeredness, and egocentrism, which are by-products of formal operational thinking, are part of the normal narcissism of adolescence; the degree of this narcissism varies from adolescent to adolescent. Mitchell explained that while such narcissism is not pathological, it profoundly affects adolescent friendships, relationships, and romantic involvements, which in turn influences not just self-understanding but also social cognition. For instance, teenagers in general desire friendship and companionship; yet, for highly narcissistic adolescents, the need for friendship exists in more compulsive surges, and it satisfies a specific set of cravings—primarily to aggrandize the self. "The motives which propel narcissistic relationships are self-serving, and as such, they are weakly concerned with the needs and rights of the relationship partner" (Mitchell, 1992, p. 74). Moreover, when narcissistic adolescents desire relationship with peers and lovers, they generally have unrealistic expectations of giving and receiving that result in dissatisfaction. As Mitchell (1992) remarked: "Problems with 'giving' and 'receiving' undermine all narcissistic relationships because narcissists know how to receive, but they are, in a very literal sense, afraid to give" (p. 74).

Mitchell's (1992) examination of normal adolescent narcissism is insightful and engaging, but it is also disquieting, primarily because of the potency and ubiquity of cultural narcissism that can exacerbate the features of this normal form of self-preoccupation. Moreover, his analysis confirmed Lasch's (1979) claim that narcissism is a continuum. At one end are most people whose displays of narcissism are innocuous and do not interfere in any dramatic way with social interaction, prosocial development, and moral conduct. At the other end of the scale are those whose narcissism is stifling and debilitating. Such people have difficulty with social interaction, especially with honoring commitments and with engaging in sincere, loving relationships that would reveal the narcissist's vulnerability. Additionally, the narcissist's moral development would also be compromised. As Mitchell (1992) observed:

> Morality, by definition, requires the alignments of one's actions and beliefs with a principle or a standard greater than oneself. Such an alignment is inherently difficult for narcissists since they tend to make decisions about moral rightness (or wrongness) according to how they affect the self. This is not to say that narcissists are immoral, or that they believe that concepts of right and wrong do not apply to them; rather, it is to say, that, by merit of their psychological makeup, narcissists choose moral viewpoints which favor their own emotional interests. Their morality is egoism blended with pragmatism; hence, when any given morality is self-serving it is clung to with a strong sense of righteousness, however, when it is no longer self-serving, or even worse, when it is condemning of one's actions, it is abandoned. (p. 72)

Most disconcerting here is not just the self-oriented perspective of narcissistic moral judgment, but that the narcissism in contemporary culture has the potential of abetting this type of egocentric thinking. As suggested earlier, if Lasch (1979) is correct about the power and pervasiveness of cultural narcissism, then these forces could easily shift the balance of energy in normal narcissistic adolescent behavior to more enduring, debilitating forms of narcissism. In being submerged in the narcissistic belief systems and self-lifeplans of contemporary magazines, movies, media, music, advertising, and related forms of pop culture, adolescents become vulnerable to the alluring facade and promises of the narcissistic lifestyle. In addition, adolescent vulnerability to narcissistic proselytizing is magnified for those teenagers whose journey towards consolidating their identity has been delayed or stretched out over time, a journey that, in addition to the appearance of formal operational thinking, is one of the hallmarks of adolescent development.

Pursuing a Consolidated Personality

The consolidation of an adolescent's identity is the end point of what Erikson (1968) described as the identity vs. identity diffusion crisis. During this time, adolescents work at establishing "a unified, holistic self-portrait that integrates the private self (or 'I') with all the various role-oriented public selves (or 'me's') that we present to other people" (Shaffer, 1994, p. 223). In the end, it is the adolescent's "way of organizing all the past and present identifications, attributes, desires, and orientations that the individual believes best represents the self" (Damon, 1983, p. 325). Some adolescents begin the quest for a consolidated identity with focus and purpose, while others are lost, distracted, and even enervated by the immensity and complexity of the task. These differences in approach are described by Marcia (1980), who categorized four general phases that teenagers pass through as they struggle to achieve identity consolidation: *identity diffusion*, where there is no serious exploration of the self and life in general, or a commitment to a belief and value system; *foreclosure*, where there is commitment without exploration; *moratorium*, where there is exploration without commitment; and *identity achievement*, where there is exploration followed by commitment. While each of these four phases vary in the degree to which self-understanding and social cognition operate, consolidation of identity requires that these two processes be engaged and cross-fertilizing. In illustrating the role of social cognition in the construction of adolescent identity, Sroufe et al. (1996) summarized Youniss's insight into this process:

> Identity involves understanding one's own unique perspective and how it relates to the perspectives of others. Arriving at this understanding can be accomplished only through social interaction. . . . Both parents and peers provide the adolescent with relationships that are useful in this process, but they tend to make different contributions. . . . (p. 549)

Research indicated that there is a dichotomy in the relative influence of parents and peers during adolescence which has strong implications for identity consolidation. During early adolescence, teenagers are particularly affected by the peer group (especially in dealing with status within the group), but parental influence is more significant in the more important decisions of education and ethics (Sroufe et al., 1996). Furthermore, Chassin and Sherman (cited in Sroufe et al.) maintained that peer influence does not replace parental influence, even though peer influence increases during these years. However, Harris (1995) argued that parents do not have as much long-term effect on the development of their child's personality as was once assumed. Despite these disparities over the relative influence of peers and parents on adolescent identity consolidation, it is clear that peer influence enlarges the potential for the culture of narcissism to infuse itself into the adolescent personality. This is not to suggest that a parent's narcissism would not influence their adolescent child's developing identity, but rather that peer influence in the context of narcissism appears to be distinctively pronounced during these years. Elkind (1984, p. 15) addressed this infusion of narcissism in his analysis of adolescent personality, particularly as it is shaped by what Elkind refers to as either *integration* or *substitution*. Examining how integration contributes to a solid identity, Elkind focused on the tandem operation of self-understanding and social cognition, an operation that is a refinement of insights and social skills first developed and exercised during childhood. He explained that exposure to an expanding collection of people and social experiences helps the adolescent understand and appreciate her own beliefs, values, and preferences. This in turn leads her to see how she is different from and similar to others. These insights guide a teenager to see that other people respond to personal affronts and insults, as well as to praise and compliments. Elkind (1984) concluded, "As a result of this process of differentiating ourselves from others, in terms of how we are alike and different from them, we gradually arrive at a stable and unique perception of ourself" (p. 16).

Elkind remarked further that this interplay between self-understanding and social cognition, as they work towards fashioning the consolidated personality, requires time as well as mentoring by parents, teachers, and other mature adults who are willing to share the insight and wisdom of their experiences. Here, such adults help adolescents ask the right questions, explain contradictions within answers, and in general make sense of the young person's past and present experiences. In contrast, adolescents whose identity is based on substitution have either not been provided this adult mentoring or it has been rejected, and instead it has been replaced by the pressures and influence of the peer group. These adolescents relinquish their own beliefs and values and, in so doing, they substitute their own with the beliefs and values of their peers. Such teen-agers are easily influenced and controlled by others because they have such a weak sense of self-definition. Instead of developing a consolidated personality, these adolescents are developing a *patchwork self* (Elkind, 1984, p. 17).

Without using the term narcissism, Elkind (1984) captured several com-ponents of the narcissistic personality in noting that adolescents who have developed an integrated sense of identity are able to delay immediate gratification to achieve long-range goals. These teenagers are also future-oriented. In contrast, patchwork teenagers who have grown by substitu-tion are present-oriented, less able to postpone immediate gratification, and easily influenced by their peers. In striving to maintain credibility, power, and status within the group, such adolescents are easy targets for the present-oriented, self-lifeplans of cultural narcissism. And once the self-aggrandizement, self-absorption, sense of entitlement, and devalua-tion of others have become internalized by the adolescent, these teenag-ers, like their narcissistic counterparts in elementary school, present nu-merous problems for teachers. In terms of character education, these young people often tend to sabotage, either intentionally or subconsciously, a teacher's efforts to develop prosocial habits of mind, moral reflection, and sensitivity to others which are the overarching purposes of most character education programs. Still, secondary school teachers, like their elementary school colleagues, should address directly how cultural narcis-sism can derail character education activities. Chapters 5, 6, and 7 will provide specific instructional strategies and activities to foster character education, while at the same time confronting those forces of cultural narcissism that are reflected in the adolescent behavior of increasing num-bers of students.

The Moral Sense and Moral Judgment

Of all the components of the moral system, the moral sense (or, in its plural form, moral sentiments) has been the most controversial and, in many ways, the least understood. Until recently, when developmental psy-chologists discovered its role in the formation of moral beliefs and con-duct, the moral sense was largely ignored by the psychological commu-nity primarily because of the difficulty of measuring and assessing emotion within the larger area of moral development (Kagan, 1994). Instead, more attention was given to the logic of moral thinking as it unfolds across phases of development (Piaget, 1965). In the past it was the philosopher who saw the moral sense as an integral component of understanding moral conduct, and this tradition can be traced as far back in Western philosophy to Aristotle's *Nichomachean Ethics* (Pangle & Pangle, 1993). During the Enlightenment, the British philosopher Hume argued that moral feeling states, not logic, comprised the wellspring of human morality. He also suggested that just one emotion, sympathy, was the requisite sentiment that explained all the other "artificial virtues" such as justice, modesty, and etiquette (Kagan, 1994, p. 123).

In American culture, Jefferson provided the earliest and clearest articulation of the moral sense. Rejecting Locke's philosophy of moral development where a person's obligations to others are defined by her rights, Jefferson believed that this perspective did not account for what he saw as a genuine benevolence that binds humans together and that transcends the benefits of mutual advantage (Pangle & Pangle, 1993). He concluded that we naturally take pleasure in helping others, especially when they are in distress "because nature hath implanted in our breasts a love of others, a sense of duty to them, a moral instinct, in short, which prompts us irresistibly to feel and to succor their distress" (Pangle & Pangle, 1993, p. 251). Jefferson contended that the emotional bond that persons feel for one another, as well as the instinctive insight that governs one's treatment of others, is, like hearing and sight, naturally present in all humankind, regardless of culture and race, with the exception of some unfortunate few. Anticipating Damon's (1995) understanding of the systemic nature of the moral system by almost two hundred years, Jefferson maintained that the development of virtues beyond the moral sense are all incidental supports, which become essential only when the moral sense is absent or truncated. "At the same time, [Jefferson] observes that the moral instinct, like the arm or the leg, can be strengthened through exercise or atrophied through disuse: Hence, the importance of moral education that will support and exercise it" (Pangle & Pangle, 1993, p. 251).

It is difficult to assess Jefferson's influence on character education as it developed during the nineteenth century. What is clear, however, is that many of the virtues espoused in Webster's *American Spelling Book* and in the McGuffey readers (e.g., duty, responsibility, cooperation, self-control) proceed as much from feeling states as they do from logic. Furthermore, the appearance of sense-based virtues in these early school books intimates Jefferson's belief that the moral sense is innate, and therefore that such sentiments found in all children, including the newly arrived immigrants and the poor, can be nurtured and refined though education.

Recently, several philosophers as well as developmental psychologists have directed their research towards examining the role of the moral sense within the process of moral development. Among the more prominent and convincing of these researchers are Wilson (1993), Kagan (1994), and Damon (1988, 1995). Kagan (1994) maintained that "there is a set of emotional states that form the bases for a limited number of universal moral categories that transcend time and locality" (p. 119). Damon (1988) agreed, adding that "[s]ome [scholars] have gone even further in claiming that moral emotions constitute the one feature of morality that unites humans from all the world's diverse cultures" (p. 13). While the operation of the moral sense may transcend cultures, each culture determines the specific form and function of the moral sentiments. The configuration of various political, economic, and social conditions within a society will determine the surface virtues that will be encouraged, whether they be physical courage, loyalty to the community, thrift, and so on. The virtues that are emphasized during any time in history will require effort to achieve; yet, they will be within the capacity of each member of the particular society (Kagan, 1994). Most importantly, the virtues "easiest to promote in others, and to defend to oneself, are those that prevent unpleasant feelings accompanying temptations to violate a standard, that mute the discomfort following a violation, and that generate pleasant emotions through practice of virtue" (Kagan, 1994, p. 119).

Examining the fine points of the moral sense in action, Kagan (1994) explained that certain unpleasant feelings or emotional responses are triggered by particular events and conditions.

> Because people do not like . . . to feel sorry for someone less privileged, or to feel guilty . . . , these unpleasant states will be classified as bad; and people will want to replace, suppress, or avoid them. The acts, motives, or qualities that accomplish these goals will be good, and, therefore, virtuous. But the specific concrete conditions that provoke these unpleasant emotions will differ with time and location; and so, too, will the specific acts and qualities that suppress them. . . . [E]ach culture and historical period presents a unique profile of provocative conditions for a few unpleasant feeling states, and special opportunities for actions that present or alleviate these states. As a result, the concrete, morally praiseworthy characteristics that are encouraged will assume different forms. . . . If the culture has a small number of impoverished citizens, it will appear to many that it is possible to eliminate poverty; and charity towards the poor will be promoted. However, if there are too many disenfranchised, as there are in India and Tibet, success will seem unattainable, and concern for the poor is likely to be replaced with celebration of a mood of detachment. In Tibet, practice of the virtue of detachment from people and material things protects each person from the unpleasantness of chronic envy, while the few with property avoid provoking jealousy in others by disguising their wealth. (pp. 120–121)

Universal Moral Sentiments

Although it is true that each culture defines the specificity of virtue in action, it should be stressed again that such virtues are anchored in a set of *emotional states* from which *moral categories* arise (Kagan, 1994, p. 119). Based on these assumptions, Kagan (1994) identified five moral sentiments or feeling states that are the foundations of virtuous action: anxiety in response to failure, disapproval, or harm; empathy towards those in distress or need; responsibility towards those one has harmed or distressed; fatigue or boredom resulting from repeated gratifications of desire; feelings of uncertainty when one confronts disparities between one's beliefs and one's actions. Wilson (1993), too, recognized several moral sentiments, although he acknowledged that there are no doubt more than the four he has identified. He maintained that sympathy, fairness, self-control, and duty are feeling states that, among other emotional states, constitute the wellspring of one's moral behavior. He also recognized the plasticity of these feeling states, indicating, for example, that "integrity derives from a combination of the more elementary senses of duty, fairness, and self-control" (Wilson, 1993, p. xiii). Most interesting here is that the foundational yet plastic nature of these four sentiments actually subsume all of the moral feeling states identified by Kagan. Equally important is the role of self-understanding and social cognition in guiding the operation of these moral feeling states. For instance, while persons may feel strongly that they have a duty to tell the truth, many would not do so "unsparingly as to wound the feelings of a beloved friend or reveal to a homicidal maniac the location of an innocent child" (Wilson, 1993, p. xiii). Ultimately, it is the interpenetration of the components of the moral system (self-understanding, social cognition, and moral sentiments) that inform moral judgment and, finally, moral action.

One of the earliest moral sentiments to surface in humans is empathy, a feeling state identified in infants just a few days old. Damon (1988) remarked that babies often cry and display related signs of distress at the sound of another infant's crying. The child hearing the crying experiences no pain of its own, but it nonetheless registers concern. "Here we see, in the primitive world of the crib, one human sharing another's burdens. This signals the advent of empathy, one of morality's primary emotional supports" (Damon, 1988, p. 14). As babies develop cognitively and emotionally throughout early childhood, feelings of empathy are refined to include the cognitive component of perspective-taking, a mental skill allowing children to discern another's psychological state as well as the other's affective condition (Damon, 1988). This refinement necessarily includes advances in self-understanding and social cognition, advances examined in the research of Emde, Biringen, Clyman, and Oppenheim (1991) which revealed distinctions between children's understanding of true moral transgressions vs. their understanding of conventional transgressions. By about 4 years of age, children are able to understand that hitting someone or not sharing (which involves perspective-taking) is more serious than picking one's nose (Sroufe et al., 1996). Children of this age are also able to experience feelings of guilt and pride which involve evaluating the self against internalized standards. Unlike younger children whose conduct is governed largely by guilt based on what parents would say or do, these older children experience a sense of guilt based on self-understanding that they have done something wrong. The guilt arises not so much from the fear of being punished as from the undermining of self-esteem caused by failure to measure up to an internalized standard (p. 384). In terms of Wilson's and Kagan's analyses of the moral sense, children experiencing guilt for such failure would be prompted to avoid such feeling states in the future. Out of a sense of duty (or responsibility) to self and others, they would be emotionally guided to practice the self-control necessary to avoid such negative feeling states in the future.

Throughout middle and later childhood, advances in cognitive development, social relationships, and emotional awareness work together in shaping the course of moral development. The complexity of this dynamic is illustrated in a hypothetical dilemma posed to children involving a fictional child who had to choose between keeping a promise to meet a best friend who needed to talk to them or going to a movie with a new playmate in the neighborhood who was also going to pay for all the candy while at the movie (Keller & Edelstein, 1993). While most of the 7-year-olds said that the child would go to the movie, almost 70 percent of the 12-year-olds said that the fictional child would keep the promise to meet the friend. The older children reflected a need to fulfill a promise (a sense of duty), to maintain a sense of loyalty towards a best friend (another sense of duty), and to resist the pleasures of a movie and free candy (a sense of self-control). Commenting on these developments in the moral sense, Sroufe et al. (1996) observed further that these older children would feel uncomfortable when they realized that their friend was at home expecting them to keep the promise. This refined moral awareness of these older children comes not just from developments in their ability to discern how their friend felt; rather "[t]hey understand other people's feelings better because of their emotional experiences in friendships and their commitment to them. A moral sense, in other words, partly derives from participation in close relationships" (p. 472).

As with a child's self-understanding and social cognition, a child's moral sense and moral judgment can be dramatically affected by cultural narcissism. For example, with the hypothetical movie dilemma cited above, a narcissistic child, "in bending the information to fit their desires" (Mitchell, 1992, p. 72), might see no need to keep the promise. Instead, the child's sense of entitlement would offset feelings of duty or loyalty to the friend and would prompt her to go to the movie, where, in also receiving free candy, her decision would confirm her feelings of grandiosity and her sense of entitlement. While this type of self-absorbed response might appear in the narcissistic personalities of children during later childhood, the incidence of such responses would increase during adolescence when a young narcissist's emotional equilibrium would be at even greater risk. Moral judgment would also be affected because, with the appearance of formal operational thinking, the complexity of moral decision-making would leave more room for narcissistic rationalizations. And this would be especially true of children already soundly influenced by cultural narcissism during their pre-teen years.

As noted earlier, one of the tasks of adolescence is the formation of a consolidated personality (Erikson, 1963), which is stimulated largely by developments in formal operational thinking. Adolescents are now able to analyze with greater precision their own thought processes as well as the thought processes of others. Engaging in hypothetical and propositional thinking (Elkind, 1984), they are able to envision a future world and how they might fit into and contribute to it. However, the task of forming a consolidated personality, along with refinements in its attending formal operational thought, frequently causes disequilibration in social relations which, in turn, can result in emotional turmoil. And this turmoil can dramatically impact on the moral sense and moral judgment.

Erikson (1963) pointed out that the adolescent mind is in a state of moratorium, "a psychological stage between childhood and adulthood, and between the morality learned by the child, and the ethics to be developed by the adult" (p. 263). Stretched between these two worlds, adolescents frequently become perplexed because they do not see the conceptual or the functional distinctions between rules and principles. This often causes them to assert that they are being treated unfairly. For example, a sixteen-year-old may perceive his parents' school-night curfew and their restrictions for using the family car as unfair when contrasted to similar guidelines more liberally applied to his more mature nineteen-year-old sister. Similarly, a sixteen-year-older may protest her single-parent's monitoring of her social and sexual behavior as unfair especially because her mother, who is engaged to be married, is involved in a loving, sexual relationship with her fiance. These perceived contradictions between rules and principles become eventually resolved as the adolescent's self-understanding and social cognition matures. But until these advances occur, these perceived breaches in fairness can influence the adolescent's exercising of the moral sentiments, particularly fairness and sympathy, in their own social circle. This is true in early adolescence when the peer-group influence is most apparent (Sroufe et al., 1996), and this is especially the case when the social disequilibration of these situations is made worse by cultural narcissism.

Dunphy (1963) suggested that adolescent peer-society is composed largely of cliques and crowds, with clique membership generally being a prerequisite for crowd membership. Cliques are close-knit groups of two or more same-sex adolescents who share intimate thoughts and problems and who go places together. Comprised of two to four cliques, a crowd is a loose and more expansive system of peer contact (Damon, 1983). Crowds also tend to be identified by the same style of dress, attitudes, interests, and so on. Clique membership tends to decrease during high school, with older adolescent bonds developing around specific friendships and romantic relationships. Despite this later drop in clique membership, participation in both cliques and crowds tends to be exclusionary. Adolescents with different clothes, musical tastes, and styles of dress are not welcomed within a specific crowd, and they certainly have trouble penetrating the social membrane of a certain clique. Describing these dynamics, Erikson (1963) observed:

> Young people can be remarkably clannish and cruel in their exclusion of all those who are 'different' in skin color or cultural background, in tastes and talents, and often in such petty aspects of dress and gesture as have been temporarily selected as the signs of an in-grouper or outer-grouper. (p. 262)

Such exclusionary conduct may be cruel; yet, the degree of cruelty is frequently heightened by adolescents whose personalities have been strongly influenced by the culture of narcissism. In bonding with other adolescent narcissists within the clique, these youngsters, in nourishing each other's feelings of grandiosity and entitlement, further inflate their own self-absorption and importance as they devalue and exclude those outside the clique-membrane. In turn, this systematic and sustained devaluation of outsiders can dramatically stifle the growth and refinement of the moral sense but especially of sympathy towards those who are different and of fairness in dealing with these outsiders.

It should be added that while the culture of narcissism may dilute the functioning of these moral sentiments, contemporary society's perspectives on and expectations of male behavior may also contribute to undermining the cultivation of sympathy among boys. As early as middle childhood, boys reflect in their behavior a greater sensitivity to gender specific behavior than do girls, who seem to display more plasticity within gender roles (Sroufe et al., 1996). And, while it is true that socialization can influence the flexibility of gender-related thinking, Pollack (1998) maintained that modern American culture continues to communicate, both consciously and subconsciously, messages that reinforce stereotypical thinking regarding boys' feelings and behaviors. One such stereotype is that boys are not empathetic. Challenging this perspective, Pollack offered evidence that boys are as empathetic as girls, and that parents and social institutions need to foster the refinement of empathy in all children, but particularly in boys. Remarking on single-parent male households, Pollack noted that men can raise and nurture male children to exhibit empathy in all social interactions. "Even when raised without a predominant female presence, boys can learn to be sensitive and to care deeply about other people, including girls, and their feelings" (p. 63). Pollack's comments implicitly support the recent research on moral feeling states (Damon, 1988, 1995; Kagan, 1994; Wilson, 1993) which argued that a child's innate moral sense can be developed and refined through guided social interaction whose moral significance is explained by adult mentors, whether they are parents, teachers, or mature siblings. Equally significant, Pollack's research, in focusing on the importance of childrearing in cultivating the moral sense, revealed once more the influence of environment. But when the social environment contains narcissistic self-lifeplans and belief systems, the development of the child's and the adolescent's moral sense can be profoundly compromised.

Appearing just a few days after birth, the moral sense, therefore, seems to be the most elemental component of the moral system. In many ways, it is the predisposition that renders possible all forms of moral conduct. As explained previously, its moral potency is given shape by societal necessity, custom, and statute. Hence, where ancient Greece valued loyalty or physical courage (requiring a sense of duty), nineteenth-century American frontier culture honored industry and charity to strangers (requiring the sentiments of sympathy, fairness, and self-control). From this rich interplay of internal moral sentiments and external social standards comes, first, the affective motivation to behave morally, and second, the end point or target of this motivation. As self-understanding and social cognition mature, authentic moral judgment appears. This is the process whereby, when faced with a moral dilemma, one deliberately and thoughtfully selects a course of action that considers the self and others, while being guided by standards that are supported by moral feeling states.

As stated previously in this chapter, a child becomes aware of standards sometimes after the middle of the second year of life (Kagan, 1994). During these months, children may point out a broken toy truck or a dismembered teddy bear. These children might bring such damaged toys to their mothers, indicating by their language and gestures that something had been done to the toys, that something was wrong. Interestingly, 2-year-olds do not respond in this fashion to all deviations from the normal, but only to those caused by actions deemed by the children as wrong or improper. These responses indicate that the children are now making inferences about the causes of these events, that someone was responsible for these broken and mutilated toys. Moreover, as adults communicate disapproval by gestures, facial expressions, and voice modulation, they communicate to their children that someone did this to the toys and that this too was wrong (Kagan, 1994). Over time, children come to see differences between conventional transgressions and moral transgressions (Emde et al., 1991). All of these developments prompt young children to internalize standards through fear and the desire not to be punished. Hence, social norms are not violated by children during early childhood because such action will result in unpleasant consequences (Hughes & Noppe, 1991).

Kohlberg (1970), whose stage theory of moral development was discussed in chapter 1, would identify the compliant behaviors of such a young child as stage 1, level 1. As the child matures cognitively, she would move up the stages in sequence; skipping stages would not occur. In their analysis of Kohlberg's model, Hughes and Noppe (1991) explained that the "stimulus for moral development is internal disequilibrium" (p. 555). As children confront higher, more refined forms of moral reasoning, they tend to internalize these modes of judgment. But they must also find these more sophisticated methods of moral examination intelligible. A teacher could enhance moral development through discussions of Kohlberg's moral dilemmas that permit students to analyze their own moral thinking by examining it in relation to others. Students would be able to refine their own moral thinking and move up to higher levels of moral understanding. Critics of this approach, however, noted that the strong emphasis on moral discussion neglected the issues of motivation and resulted in a form of *rhetorical sophistication* that permitted students the ability to rationalize their own behavior but without leading them to internalize essential moral principles (McClellan, 1992, p. 94). Ironically, adolescent-narcissists would thrive in this environment of rhetorical sophistication where, once more bending "information to fit their desires" (Mitchell, 1992, p. 72), they could rationalize their own felt qualities of perfection and entitlement as they reacted to the moral dilemmas. And "because narcissists tend to make decisions of moral rightness (and wrongness) according to how they affect the self" (p. 72), it would seem that most adolescent narcissists would have difficulty going beyond their own self-absorption as well as the egocentrism that characterizes Kohlberg's lower stages of moral thinking.

Teachers who use the moral reasoning model appear to have an affinity for using values clarification activities as warm ups or preparations for analyzing Kohlberg's moral dilemmas. Others, however, forego these moral dilemmas completely and focus entirely on Simon's seven steps of valuing described in chapter 1. At best, values clarification may force students to reflect upon what they value in their everyday lives, although Wilson (1993) thinks not, commenting that "there is no evidence that this bit of pedagogical idiocy had any effect on the beliefs of children" (p. 6). At worse, values clarification blurs distinctions between trivial preferences, such as one's favorite color, and authentic moral issues, like one's position on capital punishment (Sommers, 1984). For adolescent narcissists, however, values clarification activities provide yet another opportunity for them to be on parade, for them to publicly acknowledge what they value, why they value it, and why others should. Furthermore, for true narcissists, these public proclamations of value offer contexts for them to denigrate the values of other students, while luring other more vulnerable, identity-confused teenagers into their own value system of grandiosity, entitlement, and self-absorption.

Just as Pollack (1998) recognized how societal stereotypes misrepresent the potential of boys' emotional capacity, Gilligan (1982) argued that Kohlberg's model of moral reasoning misrepresented women's approach to moral judgment. She contended that men from infancy are guided to separate themselves from others as they form their identities. Consequently, men develop a moral code that emphasizes the rights of individuals, an *Ethic of Justice*. In contrast, from infancy women are guided to value their relatedness to others, resulting in an *Ethic of Care* that emphasizes a moral code founded on caring for and empathizing with others. As Hughes and Noppe (1991) observed:

A morality of care tends to place the value of social sensitivity above the value of abstract principles ('I would not steal from you because I do not want to hurt you' as opposed to 'I would not steal from you because I respect your property rights'). (p. 569)

Gilligan (1982) contended that Kohlberg's six-stage model describing moral development, based on a study of 84 boys whose development he tracked for over twenty years, is inadequate to describe females. She emphasized that according to Kohlberg's scale women tended to score lower than men, falling mostly at stage three. Stage three moral reasoning "is conceived in interpersonal terms, and goodness is equated with helping and pleasing others. This conception of goodness is considered . . . to be functional in the lives of mature women insofar as their lives take place in the home" (p. 18). Gilligan also maintained that according to Kohlberg, women would refine their moral judgment once they entered their world of work outside the home. This male-dominated arena would propel women into more sophisticated modes of moral reasoning "where relationships are subordinated to rules (stage four) and to universal principles of justice (stage five and six)" (p. 18).

Although the overwhelming body of research does not indicate gender differences in moral functioning (Damon, 1983; Hughes & Noppe, 1991), Gilligan's (1982) observations are significant on two accounts. First, in explaining the dynamics of the Ethic of Care, she stated that females may be more innately prosocial than are males (and there is some research to support this; for instance, McGinniss, 1985, and Sroufe et al., 1996) and that females have a deep reservoir of emotional strength from which to draw. Additional research is needed here in terms of whether women's moral sentiments actually do function more directly and forcefully than do men's within the moral system. Second, her observations are reminders that moral judgment in real-life situations is not pure abstraction that functions in an emotional vacuum. Standards that persons embrace and that guide their conduct appeal to both the heart as well as to the mind. As Kagan (1994) remarked:

Each of us is persuaded of the moral rightness of an idea by two different, incommensurate processes. One is based on feelings; the other, on logical consistency with a few deep premises. When a standard derives its strength from either foundation, we find it difficult to be disloyal to its directive. When it enjoys the support of both, as it does for torture and unprovoked murder, its binding force is maximal. (p. 124)

Ideally, this amalgam of logic and sentiments should assist teachers engaged in character education. But as explained earlier, adolescent narcissists can sabotage even the best-planned efforts. Because narcissists bend reality to support their own self-perception and their own emotional needs, and because their emotions are directed almost exclusively inward, teachers cannot assume that these adolescents will respond to more traditional character-education strategies unless these approaches concomitantly address the subversive forces of the culture of narcissism.

Chapter Four

Cultivating the Moral System through Educational Technology

What is educational technology? And, why should classroom teachers consider infusing it into their everyday classroom instruction? Heinich, Molenda, Russell, and Smaldino (1999) did not define educational technology per se; however, they do provide the analogous and useful term, *technology for learning*. In their view technology for learning is "an application of technology that aids the learning process; [it] may refer to either 'hard' technologies (communications media) or 'soft' technologies (processes or procedures that follow a technological approach)" (p. 410). Hooper and Rieber (1995) refined the concept of educational technology as being a purposeful blending or partnership of both "idea" and "product" technologies in order "to create the best learning environments for students" (p. 155). Product technologies are tangible pieces of hardware that range from high-tech digital camcorders or multimedia desktop computers with DVD-ROM drives to low-tech instruments such as colored chalk and classroom bulletin boards. Similarly, product technologies include instructional software ranging from textbooks to laserdiscs to interactive CD-ROMs. Idea technologies, on the other hand, are intangible, but are "usually represented in or through some product technology" (p. 159). Examples of idea technologies might include simulations and cooperative learning methods as well as systematic classroom activities based upon pedagogical theories such as multiple intelligences (Gardner, 1983, 1993) or mind styles (Gregorc, 1985; Guild & Garger, 1998).

Developing Professional Rationales

When in-service and pre-service teachers are questioned whether technology should be incorporated into the classroom, most respond affirmatively. They point out, for instance, that since technology is already so pervasive in contemporary society, as is increasingly evident in both the home and the workplace, it only makes sense to incorporate it into classroom instruction in order to help prepare youngsters for the rapidly changing world. Many note, additionally and with cursory reflection, that technology makes learning fun, interesting, and stimulating because it provides methodological variety in the classroom (Sweeder, 1996). A few may express legitimate concern about some children who spend too much time sitting isolated and passive in front of a television set watching cable television's *Nick at Night* or mousing away at a computer screen, indiscriminately surfing the Internet; and, invariably, one or two others muse that technology might some day replace teachers altogether in some Orwellian nightmare. Nevertheless, most think that technology's potential benefits outweigh its shortcomings.

But is it sufficient to simply use one's intuition in answering questions of this nature in order to justify technology's use in schools? Probably not. Classroom teachers not only need to refine their awareness and understanding of what educational technology means, but they also need to develop their individual professional teaching philosophies regarding the adoption and creative infusion of product and idea technology to improve teaching and learning processes and to reach more of their students more of the time.

What does professional literature on educational technology indicate regarding the improvement of teaching and learning? Much of it suggests that technology is useful in supporting multimodal approaches which, when students are engaged in learning tasks involving visual, auditory, and tactile/kinesthetic modalities, foster better understanding and retention of new concepts and skills (Guild & Garger, 1998). Similarly, in commenting upon technology's effectiveness regarding learner recall, Hofstetter (1994) reported that learners

> retain only twenty percent of what they see and thirty percent of what they hear. But they remember fifty percent of what they see and hear, and as much as eighty percent of what they see, hear, and do simultaneously. That is why multimedia [technology] provides such a powerful tool for teaching and learning. (p. 7)

Technology has also been shown to increase learner productivity, impact positively upon attitudes and achievement for both regular and special-needs students, foster student responsibility in schoolwork, encourage cooperative learning, make instruction more student-centered and stimulating, and increase student/teacher classroom interaction (Mehlinger,

1996). Electronic technologies also enable educators to "do now what was not possible before" (Peck & Dorricott, 1994, pp. 11–12). For instance, an integrated learning system (ILS) enables teachers to prescribe "individual learning paths" (p. 12) for their students, paths which, in turn, allow them to progress at their own appropriate pace. Having the capability for "continuously monitor[ing] individual learner and class performance, and provid[ing] diagnostic and prescriptive information for learners" (Mills, 1994, p. 27), an ILS is not only used for instruction, but for management as well.

Peck and Dorricott (1994) pointed out that technology fosters efficiency by allowing students to access, evaluate, and communicate information more easily and faster than ever before. They noted, additionally, that technology increases the quantity and quality of students' thinking and writing, enabling them, through an array of productivity tools, to solve higher-level complex problems. And, they acknowledged that technology nurtures artistic expression, heightens learner comfort levels with society's increasingly ubiquitous digital technology tools, fosters global awareness, produces products that have value outside of the school walls, and brings new experiences and information previously unimagined into the classroom through distance learning.

Other educators observed that technology expands student global awareness (Dyrli, 1993), creating opportunities for multiple perspective-taking and cross-age relationships (Orwig, 1995) as well as multicultural education (Gray & Herrick, 1995). Technology also addresses an especially critical societal need: enabling the disabled learner. This has been accomplished through a variety of assistive technologies. In the *ASCD Yearbook 1998: Learning with Technology*, Behrmann wrote:

> Technology can become a great equalizer for individuals with disabilities that might prevent full participation in school. . . . This is most evident in the case of individuals with mobility, hearing, or vision impairments, but is also true for individuals with limitations in cognition and perception. . . . (p. 74)

McGrath (1998) argued that technology integration has had, over the past decade, an enriching impact upon teacher-student relationships. She observed, for instance, that technology promotes positive classroom change such as increased student motivation and collaboration, more informal student-teacher interaction, and an improved "balance of power" (p. 59) in the classroom, with students accepting more responsibility for their learning and demonstrating more persistence with their problem solving. Moreover, McGrath (1998) claimed that technology fosters teacher-asfacilitator; promotes varied methods of assessment; enhances the teacher's ability to work more effectively with diverse bodies of students; encourages increased and improved oral and written communication; increases opportunities for more depth of understanding as well as for more thematic, interdisciplinary explorations; and makes classroom activities feel more real world and relevant, thus helping students to take these authentic activities more seriously. Similarly, Rose and Meyer (1994) reported that technology enables teachers and students to expand their "repertoire of tools for recording and conveying their ideas and for learning about the ideas of others. . . . [adding that] In the workplace, computers and digital media are rapidly becoming the norm" (pp. 293–294).

Moreover, educational technology addresses a wide variety of teacher and student assessment procedures such as electronic portfolio development (Milone, 1995); further, it nurtures the expanding roles of teachers as facilitators, coaches and motivators (Hancock, 1996), as well as traditional expert knowledge-givers. Technology nurtures both independent and cooperative learning activities (Peha, 1995; Grabe & Grabe, 1998); enhances distance learning opportunities (Peha, 1995); boosts student enthusiasm (Peha, 1995); increases teacher accessibility to students, parents and other caregivers; and combats teacher isolation (Dyrli, 1993). Technology also helps students develop higher order thinking skills (Hancock, 1996); provides nonjudgmental feedback (Vocational, Technical, and Adult Education, Incorporated [VTAE], 1993); promotes "creative thinking, visual literacy, and non-linear thinking" (Brown, 1993, p. 35); increases students' active, in-class participation (Hancock, 1996); and, as illustrated later in this chapter, cultivates student character by promoting prosocial behaviors and retarding narcissistic tendencies.

The Moral System: An Enlightened Idea Technology

Over the last decade and a half, Gardner's theory of multiple intelligences, as introduced in *Frames of Mind* (1983), inspired educators to explore ways of applying his theory to a wide variety of classroom settings. Briefly, Gardner maintained that all human beings possess, in varying degrees, at least eight distinct intelligences or talents. He further suggested that those intelligences need to be recognized and nurtured in some intellectually honest fashion in educational systems. Educators should not, he argued, nurture exclusively children's linguistic and logical mathematical intelligences; they should celebrate students' spatial, musical, interpersonal, intrapersonal, naturalistic, and bodily-kinesthetic talents as well, offering pupils multiple opportunities to demonstrate what they learn in school in a variety of ways (D'Arcangelo, 1997). Campbell, Campbell, and Dickenson (1996) adapted Gardner's (1983) theoretical framework, and used it systematically in order to structure a text for teachers that offers "practical classroom applications of the Theory of Multiple Intelligences" (p. xxi). Other pedagogically rich, theoretical structures such as Bloom's taxonomy of instructional objectives (Good & Brophy, 1990), Bruner's three modes of knowledge representation (Good & Brophy, 1990), Johnson and Johnson's five basic elements of cooperative learning (Kindsvatter et al., 1996), Judi Harris's telecomputing activity structures (1998), and McCarthy's 4MAT (1987) model have traditionally helped educators systematically enrich classroom instruction by providing pedagogically sound frameworks which help teachers address diverse sets of learner needs. Such frameworks can be viewed as idea technologies, systematic cognitive schemes which act as blueprints to explain abstractions.

In light of such theoretical yet practical structures for improving teaching and learning, and considering that American classrooms are becoming increasingly pluralistic, Damon's (1995) moral system, also an idea technology, can and should be incorporated into school curricula. An intangible, yet powerful, framework which holds the potential to heighten students' moral awareness levels and reduce the negative effects of cultural narcissism, Damon's moral system directly addresses not only the cognitive and social domains of student development, but the ethical dimension as well. As such, Damon's theory is an enlightened idea technology, which when infused into school curricula and blended creatively with a variety of other idea and product technologies, becomes an especially powerful pedagogical tool for character building.

In order to understand more clearly the core concepts presented thus far in this chapter, consider the graphic organizer in Figure 4.1.

Within the universe of cultural narcissism exists the world of educational technology, from which educators can select and blend numerous combinations of idea and product technologies. Notice the use of the dotted lines that separate idea from product technologies, and educational technology from the subject matter disciplines. Those lines symbolize the interpenetrating and transactional effects that those technologies have upon each other as well as the four disciplines into which those technologies can be infused. Note, too, how the subject matter disciplines listed at the bottom of Figure 4.1 are partitioned. There the dotted borderlines suggest that each discipline may be treated separately, team-taught, or combined in a comprehensive, transdisciplinary manner. The following example illustrates how Figure 4.1 might operate.

The Culture of Narcissism

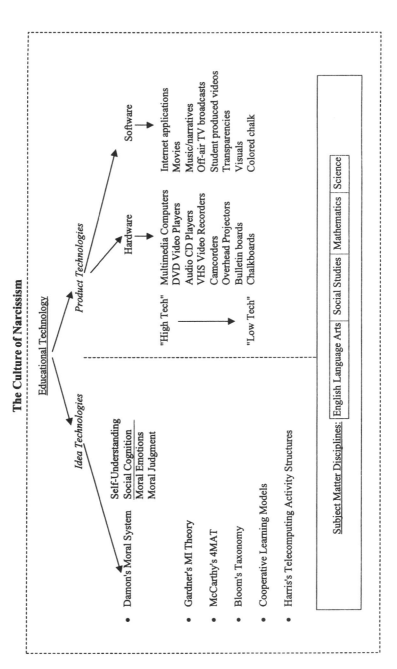

Figure 4.1 The Culture of Narcissism

A pair of high school English and social studies teachers, who are teaching the concept of civil disobedience, may utilize four idea technologies: the moral system, multiple intelligence theory, cooperative learning, and the video production process. The teachers would then blend these idea technologies with product technologies including storyboards, audio CDs, mixers, camcorders, and VHS tapes to have their classes produce a set of creative, instructional videos.

It is important to emphasize that the graphic organizer in Figure 4.1 is designed to be suggestive and descriptive, not all-inclusive or prescriptive. A plethora of idea and product technologies exist as well as a variety of other critically important school subjects, such as music, art, and physical education, which this book does not address. Nevertheless, the central purpose of this schema is to have it serve as a practical, as well as enlightened, framework for secondary pre- and in-service teachers as they fashion programs of instruction, teaching units, and daily lesson plans within and across subject matter disciplines that address issues of character development. Readers may find it especially useful to bookmark and refer to Figure 4.1 not only as they read this chapter, but also as they read the subsequent praxis chapters in Part II of this book.

Blending Damon's Moral System with Other Technologies

Classroom teachers can enhance their instruction, assist students in comprehending course content, and cultivate student character by creatively blending Damon's (1995) moral system with other forms of educational technology such as those delineated in Figure 4.1: the culture of narcissism. To illustrate, consider how Damon's four-component moral system, pairing self-understanding with social cognition, and moral sentiments with moral judgment would integrate with two of Judi Harris's (1998) telecomputing activity structures (namely, virtual gatherings and social action projects), problem-solving computer courseware like Tom Snyder's 1998 *Decisions, Decisions: The Environment* (Dockterman, 1990), and Sherman's (1991) three-stage video production process. Keep in mind, however, that each component of the moral system, whether paired or treated separately, will be maximized in function when conjoined with the other elements. Just as human bodies need the brain, heart, lungs, and digestive system to work in tandem, so, too, does the moral system need each of its four components in order to function properly.

Self-Understanding and Social Cognition: Virtual Gatherings and Sympathy

According to Harris (1995) a virtual gathering is a form of telecommunication activity that is meant to "bring together participants from different geographic locations and time zones in real-time to either participate virtually, 'in person,' in a computer-mediated meeting, or simultaneously 'in spirit,' without direct electronic contact, in similar activities at different project sites" (p. 61). Virtual gatherings appear to be ideal mechanisms for teachers to help students develop the moral sentiment of sympathy. For instance, after explaining what virtual gatherings are and discussing examples of how they have been used in other secondary classrooms across the country, teachers can have their students invent their own virtual gathering projects. One example might include having students participate in a series of activities similar to one identified by Harris as "A Day Without Art," which took place in Florida across all sixty-seven school districts in observance of the Eighth Annual World AIDS Day (1995). Using a combination of Internet Relay Chats and a preorganized symbolic action targeting the removal of blindfolds from museum statuary, "A Day Without Art" helped not only to develop AIDS awareness, but also to engender sympathy for the welfare of those afflicted with that life-threatening disease.

After participating in "A Day Without Art," teachers could subsequently conduct debriefing sessions in which they pose questions for their students such as, How might you feel if a close family member, a friend, or you, yourself, contracted this disease accidentally through a blood transfusion? How would you expect or wish to be treated? In what ways could you lend support to ease the burden of suffering or anxiety? What role, if any, do you think the government should play in providing treatment for AIDS patients or in funding AIDS research? Such questions recall Baldwin's (1902) observations regarding the reciprocal function of self-understanding and social cognition. As students are led to decenter and thoughtfully consider the plight of others, they gain insight into the self regarding their position in relation to larger global issues. Further, in discussing such questions students may not only refine their thinking and metacognition, which again enhances self-understanding, but also generate additional questions that may subsequently lead to self-inspired research within or across a variety of disciplines. For example, they may ask: What percentage of the world's population is HIV-positive (mathematics)? What exactly is HIV? Is it different from AIDS? How does HIV spread (science)? What is the government doing to prevent the diffusion of this disease?

What can we do to help (social studies)? To whom can we write to express our opinions regarding this problem (English language arts)? Here again, these questions require the hypothetical mode of formal operational thought. These speculations, when properly mentored, can assist students with identity formation and with their subsequent understanding of the plight of others.

Harris's virtual gathering activity structure can serve as a template for other ways in which teachers might develop student awareness for the moral sentiment of sympathy: Why not "A Day Without TV," in order to spend some time visiting and talking to the elderly or infirmed, or "A Day Without Dessert" in order to devote time collecting food for the homeless? Using curriculum-specific topics as springboards, science, English language arts, or mathematics teachers could foster content mastery and technology use while simultaneously nurturing moral awareness (Ryan, Bednar, & Sweeder, 1999).

Self-Understanding and Social Cognition:
The Social Action Project and Duty

Teachers can also use the Internet to help students tap into a variety of real world contexts for altruistic, action-oriented telecommunications activities that involve children reaching out beyond the classroom in order to solve down-to-earth problems. Social action projects may range from helping raise money in aiding the homeless, to organizing, scheduling, and conducting worldwide beach sweeps in order to "Save the Earth's Beaches" (J. Harris, 1998, p. 42). By participating in such activities, students, our future world leaders, would discover that they are not powerless bystanders: they can effect change, especially if they mobilize. Such projects help students develop an individual sense of empowerment (which leads to deeper self-understanding) as well as a collective pride, a pride that is nurtured when important problems are solved together, when responsibility is shared (which enhances social cognition).

Technology-infused projects of this nature can also be used to address traditional curricular concerns and heighten students' moral consciousness in order to develop a communal, if not universal, sense of duty to humanity. For example, in math classes, students might calculate how many pounds of refuse would actually be needed in order to raise enough money to feed and clothe groups of homeless people located in community shelters. In English classes, students might design a school web page inviting other schools to join and coordinate their civic efforts. In science classes, children could learn how to differentiate among several types of refuse, recognizing that some forms of trash are less biodegradable than other forms, and thus are environmentally more hazardous to future generations. Social studies teachers might have their classes focus upon the political dimensions of these projects by helping students create their own electronic polling instrument designed to collect data that would then be analyzed. Such information would help adolescents identify and prioritize important social problems which, in the view of like-minded distant peers, they would subsequently address.

Moral Sentiments and Moral Judgment: Decisions, Decisions and Fairness

Another way middle and secondary school teachers can help enrich their students' moral systems would be through the careful selection and repurposing of computer courseware. For example, Tom Snyder's *Decisions, Decisions: The Environment* (Dockterman, 1990) and its accompanying teacher's guide (Dockterman, 1988) are primarily intended to improve pupil decision-making and critical thinking skills, both leading to refining self-understanding and social cognition. However, with a modicum of creativity, classroom teachers can readily adapt this product technology in order to develop their students' moral sense of fairness as pupils mete out justice that is based upon the needs and perspectives of others.

In *Decisions, Decisions: The Environment*, students are encouraged via small and large group collaboration, multiple perspective-taking, and role-playing simulations to analyze and solve a real-life situation: What is causing fish to die in the local pond? Playing the role of the mayor of Alpine, students are asked not only to solve this multifaceted problem, but also to take into consideration the advice of four mayoral advisors: an independent scientist, an economist, a campaign manager, and a representative of an environmental council. In addition, the mayor has to weigh and balance a number of other complicating circumstances, such as preserving the valuable jobs which are at stake at the local mining company, a company which may be the possible source of the pond's pollution problem. All of this takes place during a crucial election year. Faced with competing agendas from the various mayoral advisors, students directly confront the complexity inherent in civic decision making and ultimately are required to prioritize these agendas according to their respective moral belief systems. While this software program demonstrates that fairness is indeed complex, the activity would ideally prompt the student mayors to see that the scientist, economist, campaign manager, and environmental advocate should work together in cleaning up the polluted pond. In nudging the students in this direction, teachers would assist them in weighing "equality, merit, need and other social concerns in reaching decisions about fairness. In addition, empathetic concerns for another's feelings, and pragmatic concerns about the consequences of not sharing [should] both continue to weigh heavily" (Damon, 1988, p. 42).

While *Decisions, Decisions: The Environment* may seem to be tailored for a social studies or science curriculum, English and mathematics teachers can similarly plug this piece of exciting courseware into their classroom instruction. English teachers, for example, could help learners construct thematic analogies by having students concurrently read Upton Sinclair's classic work, *The Jungle*, or attend a production of Henrik Ibsen's drama, *An Enemy of the People*, or view James Bridges's 1979 film *China Syndrome* as well as excerpts from Mike Nichols's 1983 *Silkwood*. Math teachers might recommend that students conduct some exploratory research, interviewing local insurance providers (perhaps via a combination of personal visitations, voice mail, or e-mail correspondences), experts who are familiar with what math is needed, for example, in assembling, calculating, and graphing actuarial tables. Such experiences would not only be academically engaging and culturally enriching, but also perspective enhancing and morally enlightening.

Moral Sentiments and Moral Judgment: Video Production and Self-Control

Teachers can have learners cultivate the moral sentiment of self-control through the incorporation of video production projects into classroom lessons. By experiencing the three-stage, videographic process (preproduction, the "shoot" itself, and postproduction) students, under an instructor's tutelage, ascertain the five basic elements of cooperative learning (Kindsvatter et al., 1996). Taken together, those elements deal with the establishment, maintenance, and promotion of interpersonal relationships. An important aspect of any challenging, collaborative endeavor such as the creation of a coherent "movie story" (Sherman, 1991) necessitates self-control and the ability to compromise, especially at a video project's outset, the preproduction phase, when themes, plots, characters, dialogue, responsibilities, and so on are being invented and determined collectively. Compromise, by definition, involves the settlement of individual differences, at least in the short run, in order to permit a project to move forward, prosper, and meet the longer-range goals of the group: a completed, creative, and coherent video. Compromise also requires

Video Project: Assessment Rubric

<u>Group Members:</u>   _____

_____

_____

_____

4 = Superior Work: A model for others to emulate
3 = Very Good: Fulfilled all requirements in a competent manner
2 = Satisfactory: Fulfilled most requirements, but problems or omissions still exist
1 = Unsatisfactory: Did not meet the minimum requirements

_____. *The process*: demonstrated collaborative support, individual accountability, effort, enthusiasm, and the ability to meet deadlines.

_____. *The storyboard and/or rundown sheet*: demonstrated creativity, detail, and appropriateness. The storyboard and rundown sheets made sense in and of themselves. They indicated a clear beginning, middle, and end. They possessed an identifiable central theme, which was audience appropriate.

_____. *The product*: demonstrated pictorial continuity and evidence of videographic literacy (e.g., stable shots, use of tripod, slow pans and tilts, minimal zooms, varied angles, use of basic shots, cut-aways, cut-ins, subjective camera, reaction shots, proper headroom, pacing, clean entrances and exits, and so on); audio: demonstrated appropriate use of music, V.O., sound effects, or a combination thereof.

_____. *The group-assessment*: provided a neatly typed reflective analysis that discussed, with a sufficient degree of depth and clarity, the strengths and shortcomings of your *product* as well as your *process*. Suggestions for revisions were also noted. Incorporated the videographic lexicon you have learned.

Overall Grade: _____

Figure 4.2 Video Project: Assessment Rubric

perspective taking, the ability to see problems from other points of view. Teachers need to help learners stand back from the demands of the project, targeting tasks to be completed and identifying respective student talents in completing these tasks. In guiding students to address these issues, teachers can foster not just self-control but also duty and fairness to the self as well as the group.

Moral judgment, the capacity to make evaluative choices for the benefits of others regarding matters of justice, care, and truthfulness can also be nurtured by conjoining the idea technologies of video production and cooperative learning. To illustrate, Kindsvatter et al. (1996) stated that the fifth of five basic elements of cooperative learning is "ensurance that groups process their achievement and maintenance of effective working relationships" (p. 308). One way teachers can directly address this element is to have each member of a small cooperative learning group carefully reflect upon and assess the completed movie stories as well as the entire videographic process itself, a process that led to the successful (or unsuccessful) completion of their final products. For instance, students could be required to compose an essay or create an audiotape detailing how well they fulfilled their individual and collective responsibilities. Classroom teachers may even provide students with a formal rubric, such as the one provided in Figure 4.2, to serve as guidepost.

Blending Idea and Product Technologies:
The Tangible and Intangible

Technology implies the use of specific components, elements, and/or psychological constructs as part of a systematized method of accomplishing a task. An idea technology is a cognitive schema which acts as a blueprint to explain and operationalize an abstraction. A product technology is the tangible result of an idea technology. Thus Henry Ford's conceptualization of the production of cars is an idea technology; whereas, the actual assembly line is the resulting product technology (Hooper & Rieber, 1995). An idea technology is systemic in that the elements within the idea can move about and influence each other. In this context, the moral system is an idea technology. For example, as students examine how the moral emotion of fairness operates in their lives, they concurrently may come to see how the sentiments of duty and sympathy interact with their understanding and practice of fairness. Similarly, a product technology is also systemic (Ryan, Bednar, & Sweeder, 1999). While idea and product technologies are in themselves systemic, it is possible for teachers to enhance further the systemic nature of each by infusing the two types of technologies, thereby creating the additional benefit of dialectical cross-fertilization. For example, when teachers use educational technology to foster the moral system, students may more easily see how its four components are related to each other. Similarly, as students gain familiarity with using software packages and the Internet, their level of mastery gradually improves, thus prompting them to search out other programs and use them across the curriculum. This dialectical cross-fertilization can surface for both teachers and students as each group discovers how different their understandings of how the components of the moral system (self-understanding, social cognition, moral emotions, and moral judgment) operate in a variety of contexts and disciplines, from science and mathematics to social studies and English language arts.

Why Incorporate Educational Technology?

The infusion of educational technology into classroom instruction does not necessarily make it meritorious. Simply because children work in video production teams, interact with multimedia computer courseware, and engage in social action telecommunication projects, it does not necessarily follow that student moral systems are going to develop and flourish. Indeed, individual students may use technology, intentionally or unintentionally, in socially inappropriate ways, from pirating videos or computer software programs, to downloading copyrighted feature films or popular music from the Internet (Bitter & Pierson, 1999; Burke, 1999; Hamilton, 1999). Therefore, teachers need to remain especially cognizant of the vital role that they play in orchestrating teaching and learning processes and creating caring, respectful, and trusting classroom environments.

Technology neither can, nor should, replace teachers. It is not technology alone that can increase student academic achievement; rather it is how, and in what context, teachers use that technology that matters. For example, when technology-trained fourth and eighth grade math teachers used computers to teach students higher order thinking skills, as opposed to drill and practice methods, academic gains were much larger, especially for the eighth graders (Latham, 1999). Likewise technology can be used to foster all components of the moral system. However, once more the teacher's role is critical in guiding students to use technology appropriately in developing their self-understanding and social cognition as well as in using it to engender their moral sentiments and to refine their moral judgment. But given the potency of normal adolescent narcissism, which is often amplified by narcissistic culture, high school teachers are especially challenged in directing students to appreciate how such narcissism can ultimately compromise the workings of the moral system.

Two Additional Issues

As we conclude Part I of this book and move forward to Part II, the Praxis chapters, we need to address two additional, ethically related issues pertaining to teachers and technology. The first deals with acknowledging the fact that a "paradigm shift" (Tapscott, 1998, p. 24) in human communications continues to emerge; thus, teachers must not only attend to this shift, but also be willing to adjust and balance some of their instructional approaches in light of it. Equally important, the second issue deals with the exigency of resolving the information technology "access gap" (Latham, 1999) or "digital divide" (Tapscott, 1998), which continues to widen within and among our nation's schools, school teachers, and school children.

A Paradigm Shift to New Media

Are tomorrow's adolescents predestined to drown in a culture of narcissism for the foreseeable future? Can American society transform itself technologically while diminishing its obsession with self-absorption? Does American society have any imminent cause for optimism? Futurist Tapscott (1998) suggested that we indeed have reason for optimism. Recently, he asserted that children born after 1977, those he has dubbed the Net Generation, spend less time watching television than their predecessors and devote increasingly more time computing on-line, interacting with the new media (i.e., personal, networked multimedia computers). Often engaged in prosocial if not altruistic behaviors, *N-Gen* teenagers, Tapscott claimed, are active multitasking computer users, not passive TV viewers, who "care deeply about social issues" (p. 9). Contrasting the N-Geners with the self-absorbed baby boomers and Generation Xers, Tapscott asserted that the former group "have a great desire to be connected with others[,] especially with family and close friends, in schools, neighborhood, interest groups, and online in . . . virtual communities" (p. 287).

N-Geners not only care, they are doing more to try to change things. According to the Higher Education Research Institute at the University of California at Los Angeles, in 1996 a record 72 percent of freshman reported having performed volunteer work "frequently" or "occasionally" during the past year. (p. 288)

If Tapscott's conclusions are valid, we may, indeed, be embarking upon a revolutionary "paradigm shift" that offers opportunities for classroom teachers to explore innovative ways to help children capitalize upon the cybernetic possibilities of fostering pro-social behavior while reducing cultural narcissism.

Foiling "Information Apartheid"

Ironically, despite the "significant increase in the number of microcomputers . . . purchased for home use" (Bitter & Pierson, 1999, p. 255), many educational leaders, particularly those representing students who come from economically disadvantaged families in urban and rural school districts, protest that they desperately need to infuse technology into their schools' curriculums. Moreover, those leaders maintain that there is not only insufficient capital for purchasing sufficiently powerful, Internet ready computers, but also for restructuring aging, factory-modeled, plant infrastructures that still exist in the computer age. And so teachers ask on behalf of their students, especially those who are often labeled at-risk: What do we do if we live in a high-tech world, but work in a low-tech school district? The "access gap," the gap between the "haves" and the "have-nots" (Dusick, 1998), has not only fractured, but has further widened and developed into an "information apartheid" (Tapscott, 1998, p. 259) as electronic portals to knowledge have become increasingly vital in the global, networked, information-rich world.

In order to deal with this digital divide, we believe, as Tapscott does, that "Every institution and every person will need to get involved" (p. 265). We need to develop pro-social solutions, ones that include seeking private, state, and federal grant money for much needed teacher retraining; putting new or used portable laptop computers in the hands of teachers and students so they can not only transport them from classroom to classroom, but also from school to home if need be; applying for government "e-rate" reductions in order to diminish phone charges for school Internet connections; forming partnerships with local businesses and nearby universities to share resources; and fostering community volunteerism by developing programs that encourage neighborhood seniors to donate their time at the school helping to supervise adolescents and learn with them as they acquire technological skills.

Perhaps, too, Tapscott's caring, computer savvy N-Geners would be more than willing to donate some of their time in order to help the "have-not" school districts get up-to-speed more quickly on the information superhighway by volunteering to set up, connect, and troubleshoot new or used hardware, and by offering to tutor computer "newbees"—teachers, administrators, and students—in the basic set up and operation of the networked computer. Such community service, whether performed on-site in-person, or virtually on-line, would bolster adolescents' moral systems and help build character.

Bridge to Praxis

Chapters 1 through 4 have presented our central argument: that character education should be repositioned to a more central place within the school curriculum and that recent research in the moral system can provide the needed direction for doing so. The opening chapters also explained how the forces of cultural narcissism can thwart efforts to engage successfully in character education in secondary school classrooms as well as to engender many of the prosocial behaviors on which such character education is based. To complete the argument, chapter 4 examined how idea and product technologies can be blended in classroom instruction to nurture various components of the moral system and to combat the negative elements of cultural narcissism.

The following chapters, referred to as Praxis, will provide instructional models for infusing character education into typical secondary-level classrooms. Chapters may include a sample unit on a selected theme within the academic discipline and/or shorter "snapshot" suggestions that can be utilized in two- or three-day segments. In particular, Chapter 5, "Character Education in the English Language Arts Classroom," will feature a unit on Hamlet and Identity. Chapter 6, "Character Education in the Social Studies Classroom," will present a unit on immigration, multiculturalism, and identity, with additional models on teaching American social history, geography, and historical biography. Chapter 7, "Character Education in the Mathematics and the Science Classroom," will focus on algebra classes where graphing calculators are used for plotting variables, while the science component features a biology unit on heredity where the major emphasis is placed on the culminating problem-solving projects.

All of these models have been developed in ways that are sensitive to the demands and realities of daily classroom instruction. They can be modified in numerous ways, either through compression or extension.

The time constraints of the sample units have been loosened to accommodate either the traditional 40- or 50-minute secondary-level period or the longer block-scheduled pattern. This is also why some suggested activities within the respective units are listed as varying in length over two or more days. Ultimately, the teacher as decision maker will control the application and general use of the strategies and the time required for student engagement with the content and the activities. Above all, these models will emphasize the teaching of the academic content as primal, with infusions of prosocial awareness and character development as appropriate and as logical extensions of both content and pedagogy.

Because the language and concepts endemic to each academic subject are different, the respective approaches for doing character education in each chapter will draw on these different concepts and language use. Despite the linguistic and conceptual distinctions that separate, for instance, English from social studies, and each of these from mathematics and science, there are numerous aspects of the daily teaching enterprise that are common to all secondary school classrooms. Furthermore, these generic aspects of classroom life offer opportunities for cultivating prosocial awareness and for refining the moral system. Three of these generic features—instruction, management and discipline, and student assessment—can foster character education indirectly through the hidden curriculum, while other features, as they relate to character development, may be stressed more overtly by the teacher.

Instruction

While teachers may have preferences for using either transmissive or constructivist methodology, most teachers today tend to use both approaches, with differences between instructional styles reflected in the degree to which teachers blend one approach with the other (Hooper & Rieber, 1995). Regardless of the mix of strategies, both types of instruction provide opportunities for cultivating the moral system. For example, teacher-led recitations can guide students to a deeper understanding of themselves as individuals and about others as well. These insights can be reinforced or extended through written worksheets and/or through journal assignments. Similarly, various configurations of cooperative learning can result in both heightened self-understanding and social cognition. Through direct instruction, teachers can also offer examples and situations that stir up students' moral sentiments and can then guide students to apply these sentiments in making moral judgments. Likewise, through role-play, simulations, video productions, and related cooperative learning activities, teams of students can have their moral emotions stimulated and then used as springboards to begin evaluating the moral appropriateness of human conduct.

Management and Discipline

Depending upon their age, maturity, and level of insight, most students are aware of the need for good order, rules, and structure in the classroom. They understand that certain rules are in place for safety (e.g., do not touch the windows or the electric outlets), while others are required for efficiency and order (e.g., procedures for collecting homework, for going to the nurse's office, and for appropriate participation in classroom discussion). Once more, adherence to these rules and regulations provides students insight into themselves, which fosters self-understanding, and into others, which enhances social cognition. And while most students will acknowledge the need for specific rules, regulations, and protocols, they are likewise sensitive to breaches of fairness when the rules are applied inconsistently. Consequently, teachers must be vigilant about the fair application of rules and the use of justice in disciplining students for rule breaking. Thus, before launching into instruction and related classroom activities that are grounded in rules and regulations, teachers should engage students in a dialogue at the beginning of the school year that focuses on the following: the need for rules and regulations, how rules will be applied, and how extenuating circumstances, known only to the teacher, might be misunderstood by students as breaches of fairness. Within such dialogue, teachers should stress that insisting on rules and procedures is not something that is done "to students" but rather it is something that is done "for students" (Kindsvater, Wilen, & Ishler, 1996). Teachers might also consider having the class generate additional regulations for classroom management and discipline, resulting in student ownership of the policies as well as in refinements, once again, in self-understanding and social cognition (Edwards, 1993; Froyen & Iverson, 1999). As part of this dialogue, teachers should consider making references to mutual respect as well as to the moral sentiments (sympathy, duty, fairness, self-control) to enrich student understanding of the rules and to provide contexts for later learning when the moral system is applied to instructional activities within specific disciplines.

Assessment

Assessment, which completes the learning cycle, has been described as one of the "onerous chores of teaching" (Kindsvatter et al., 1996, p. 329). It includes writing and grading of tests, evaluating papers, reports, and projects, and assessing student participation and classroom interaction. On one level, assessment informs students where they have hit or missed an expected level of content mastery, and on another level, it guides teachers to refine their techniques of instruction and motivation, their selection of activities, and even their actual methods of assessment. However, on yet another level, assessment has direct implication for stimulating the moral system and for nurturing character development.

Whether through letter grades, written narratives, or private conferences, teachers can assist students in refining their self-understanding and social cognition by directly or indirectly raising several issues with their students: Did you exercise self-control and duty in budgeting sufficient study time? Did you demonstrate care in note-taking and outlining and in reading assignments closely and critically? Did you exhibit responsibility in group work by contributing sincerely and appropriately and by assisting other team members when the need arose? Ironically, in addressing these concerns students not only refine the components of their moral systems, but they can also stimulate their metacognition: their self-reflection about understanding the content and the studying process itself. Such metacognitive analysis can clearly result in improved achievement. These metacognitive insights can be prompted by summative assessment, which occurs at the completion of a unit of instruction; however, formative assessment, which occurs within the unit and which serves primarily a diagnostic function, is especially helpful in effecting metacognitive insight and in refining various elements of the moral system. Formative evaluation, which fundamentally answers the question "How am I doing?" (Kindsvatter et al., 1996, p. 349), provides students opportunities for midstream adjustments based upon their own assessments of content mastery and their study techniques—all of which enlarge self-understanding. And in providing a context for study groups, formative assessment can sharpen social cognition as well. Teachers, too, can profit from such assessment, for it provides them data for readjusting their approaches to instruction.

As will be described in greater detail below, teachers are multidimensional role models for their students. Within the assessment process, teachers should exhibit the consistency and fairness that they expect from their students. Tests should reflect what was covered, and clear rubrics, also shared with the class well before assessment begins, should be applied professionally. Teachers should also demonstrate duty and sympathy in devising alternative means of assessment, for instance, oral tests and quizzes, multimedia projects, portfolios, and so on, to meet the learning styles of their students, and particularly to address special-needs learners. Finally, teachers should demonstrate compassion in assessing the achievement of students who have been extensively ill or who have suffered a family death or other disaster. In all of these contexts, appropriate teacher behavior can influence student moral system development.

Teacher as Role Model

One of the most significant concepts that weaves together classroom instruction, management, and assessment is the role of the teacher. In all three processes, the teacher's decision-making skills are central in selecting effective and appropriate strategies that will challenge students, maintain order, and evaluate student mastery of material. Yet, at every turn within these processes, the teacher as decision-maker is likewise a model. As Ryan and Bohlin (1999) pointed out, students are very perceptive, noticing how teachers dress and how they behave. Extending this to the moral domain, it is critical that teachers themselves reflect behavior that fosters their students' moral systems. For example, teachers should exhibit prosocial behavior in their interaction with each student and in their relationships to all other teachers and staff members—behavior that emphasizes caring, kindness, sharing, helpfulness, and cooperation. In particular, teachers should reflect Wilson's moral sentiments (sympathy, fairness, duty, and self-control), for here, too, students are observant. Just as students can recognize that "Mrs. P. is wearing her Friday jumper" (Ryan & Bohlin, 1999, p. 141), they can just as quickly notice that Mrs. P. is not adequately prepared to teach the lesson today, a clear breach of her duty to her students.

Similarly, because teachers project such power within the classroom, they should wield this power compassionately, judiciously, and professionally. In exercising moral judgment, and especially public displays of such judgment, teachers as models of behavior must be aware of the effects of their decisions on students as individuals and on the class in general. Such decisions (e.g., how to handle a student's allegation of stolen property, or an allegation of a racial slur) have the potential of either fostering or impeding students' self-understanding as well as their social cognition. And these decisions, when grounded in Wilson's moral sentiments, constitute an object lesson that can nurture the entire moral system. Finally, all students, as well as all adults within the school, must recognize the systemic, interactive effects of their individual actions. As Ryan and Bohlin (1999) urged, "[t]he school must become a community of virtue in which responsibility, hard work, honesty, and kindness are modeled, taught, expected, celebrated, and continuously practiced" (p. 191).

Applying the Full Moral System

The instructional models that follow in the next three chapters are designed to teach academic content, while refining the moral system and countervailing the negative forces of cultural narcissism. Whenever possible, the models address all components of the moral system: self-understanding, social cognition, moral sentiments, and moral judgment. It should be noted, however, that Damon (1995) in his analysis of the moral system indicated that "the four processes [of the moral system] continuously interpenetrate all throughout the course of development, spurring each other's growth" (pp. 133–134). He then added that "[j]ust as importantly, they provide *redundancy* to the moral system. Where one process fails, another intercedes to ensure the moral act" (p. 134, italics in text).

Given the pervasiveness, endurance, and power of cultural narcissism, we are more cautious than Damon in believing in the redundancy of the moral system. As Lasch explained (1979), contemporary Western culture has been shaping a personality type that is marked by, among other traits, self-absorption, grandiosity, a sense of entitlement, and devaluation of others. Considering that such culturally formative forces are at work in society, it is no surprise that so many adolescents, many of whom already display characteristics of normal adolescent narcissism (Mitchell, 1992), are indeed vulnerable to the proselytizing of these self-lifeplans. Consequently, to offset these forces of negative narcissism, we argue that whenever possible, teachers should foster and refine all four components of the moral system through both the hidden curriculum and instructional strategies. Simply stated, given the dramatic increases in adolescent violence, bullying, grandiosity, and general disregard for others inside and outside the classroom, educators must not overlook any opportunities to develop in their students prosocial dispositions and conduct.

PART II

PRAXIS

Chapter Five

Character Education in the English Language Arts Classroom

Among the many challenges that English Language Arts (ELA) teachers face is *covering the content* while concurrently meeting professional National Council of Teachers of English/International Reading Association standards (NCTE/IRA, 1996) within a finite period of time. Veteran teachers recognize this as a *sine qua non*. Teachers, therefore, may question how to add one more variable to an already robust program of study. This challenge can be accomplished not by covering the curriculum but by thoughtfully refocusing and rearranging it. Doing this engenders opportunities for teachers to address not just the specific content but also to present timely opportunities for students to explore the moral system and cultural narcissism. Burke (1999), a high school teacher and writer, recognizes that "the English curriculum challenges both teacher and student to enter into a conversation about those moral issues that arise within the context of the stories we read together" (p. 257).

The purpose of this chapter is to help ELA teachers discover for themselves ways in which they can incorporate character education into their ELA classrooms while simultaneously navigating the curricular demands and scheduling constraints as well as the joys of their jobs, including love of content, student-teacher interactions, and creative decision-making. This chapter offers a model, not to emulate verbatim, but to serve as a point of departure, recognizing full well the wide diversity of variables all teachers face, variables ranging from the nature of the students themselves to the communities in which they learn.

Narrative Template

Through thematic units using a careful selection of print, nonprint, and electronic texts, ELA teachers can help adolescents learn about themselves. This chapter's template is a unit entitled *Quest for Identity*. Identity is chosen as a core concept for its universality and developmental appropriateness (Erikson, 1963; Hubley, 1975), as well as its compatibility with both tandems of Damon's (1995) moral system: self-understanding and social cognition; moral emotions and moral judgment (see chapter 3). In addition, the identity theme addresses the NCTE/IRA Standard One, which states:

> Students read a wide range of print and nonprint text to build an understanding of texts, *of themselves* [italics added], and of the cultures of the United States and the world; to acquire new information; to respond to the needs and demands of society and the workplace; and for personal fulfillment. Among these texts are fiction and nonfiction, classic and contemporary works. As Erikson points out teenagers in all cultures go through the identity vs. identity role diffusion stage at this time. (pp. viii–ix)

Student Population

The *Quest for Identity* ELA unit is designed to be adapted for tenth through twelfth graders, who populate American, British, or world literature programs (or a contemporary hybrid such as American studies). However, the unit described simulates a classroom full of high school juniors enrolled in a world literature class using daily 45-minute blocks of time. The unit lasts four to six weeks depending upon a variety of variables such as scheduling, student ability level, time of year, availability of academic resources, and so on. Experienced teachers know that expecting students to complete their assigned readings for homework on a regular basis is at best tenuous. Therefore, although readings are assigned to be completed at home, accommodations will be made during class periods for students who may lack the academic or motivational resources to accomplish the independent assignments.

Prior to this *Quest for Identity* unit, students completed a poetry unit where they explored traditional elements related to verse such as meter, rhythm, and rhyme as well as a variety of figures of speech and tropes such as metaphor and onomatopoeia. This is the third year that students have encountered Shakespeare, and they have a working knowledge of his times and works. For example, they have read *Julius Caesar* and *Macbeth*. In addition, students participate in an ongoing electronic writing portfolio, replete with accompanying assessment rubrics. The writing portfolio also addresses NCTE/IRA Standards 4, 5, 6 and 12 (1996).

Instructional Materials and Educational Technology

Course Content

To explore issues of identity through the lens of Damon's moral system, the unit includes an array of literature across a variety of genres and media. Such works may include Shakespeare's *The Tragedy of Hamlet, Prince of Denmark* (1957) or *Romeo and Juliet* (1964), Chopin's "The Story of an Hour" (1981), Bambara's "A Girl's Story" (1993), Dickinson's "I'm Nobody" (1959), Young's song *Rockin' in the Free World* (1989), or Simpson, Bruckheimer, and Smith's film *Dangerous Minds* (1995). Works will vary to reflect individual school district curriculum. Visits to both traditional print and electronic versions of periodicals, newspapers, and other resources such as *Newsweek*, *New York Times*, and the Internet's Discovery.com and CNN.com provide examples of expository texts to extend and enrich such a unit. Specific works for the following unit include "The Story of an Hour," "A Girl's Story," *Hamlet,* and *Dangerous Minds*, with the major instructional and assessment emphasis on *Hamlet*, the central work of the unit.

Hamlet (1957) is a frequently required drama for grades 9 through 12 (Applebee, 1992). Most ELA teachers traditionally focus upon elements of the play such as setting, plot, character development, major conflicts, theme, use of literary devices, blank verse, and so on. More often than not, the life of Shakespeare, a history of the times, and aspects of the Globe Theater are included. Typically such a unit would culminate in either a production of the play or a visit to a local theater troupe. But more importantly, this drama provides rich opportunities for students to explore and refine their own ethical development by vicariously analyzing the protagonist's search for his own identity as he encounters a series of conflicts. Like the students themselves, Hamlet embarks upon a quest, a personal journey of self-discovery, which develops through the interplay of self-understanding, social interaction, and moral decision-making within a specific milieu. Other major characters such as Ophelia, Polonius, Laertes, Claudius, and Gertrude, through their commissions and omissions, provide additional opportunities for students to explore aspects of their own character development as well as the moral system itself.

The following unit plan is meant to be suggestive not prescriptive. Each lesson or set of lessons includes brief descriptions of instructional procedures for pre- or in-service teachers to consider. The *Hamlet* lesson plans contain more detailed explanations of how to incorporate both idea and product technologies. The rationale explicating how the educational technology chosen addresses the interaction between the play's theme and the moral system appears at the unit's conclusion.

Educational Technology

The unit includes a range of educational technologies (see chapter 4, Figure 4.1), blending both ideas and products. In addition to Damon's moral system, specific references are made to idea technologies such Dodge's (1999) WebQuest, Burke's (1999) "notes and quotes," Ogle's (1989) The Know, Want to Know, Learn Strategy (K-W-L+), and Gardner's (1983, 1999) multiple intelligence theory. Among the more frequently used product technologies are videotapes and DVDs, audiocassettes, overhead transparencies, CD-ROMs, World Wide Web sites, 35MM slides and photos, chalkboards, and flipcharts. Computer software includes *PowerPoint*, *Word,* and *Inspiration*, reviewed in *Technology & Learning* (August, 1999) as "a visual learning tool for creating graphical organizers, planning, brainstorming, organizing thoughts, and mapping out multimedia projects" (p. 45).

Unit Plan: *Quest for Identity*

Week One

Monday. Begin the set induction (Allen & Ryan, 1969) of the unit by introducing the identity theme using an excerpt from the DVD videodisc entitled *Dangerous Minds* (Simpson & Bruckheimer, 1995). The characters in the film present clear-cut examples of adolescents involved in a narcissistic culture: a group of students who have repeatedly driven teachers from the classroom by their gross misbehavior, exhibitionist displays, and teacher devaluation. After viewing the videodisc, begin an interactive lecture (Kindsvatter et al., 1996) with questions which elicit responses related to the theme of identity such as: Why do the students portrayed in the video behave the way they do? Who are the leaders and followers? Who's in charge of the classroom? Probe student responses by varying questioning levels (Kindsvatter et al., 1996). As the discussion unfolds, introduce and define the moral sentiments of empathy, duty, fairness, and self-control. Connect student observations about the film's characters, which are listed on a whiteboard, flipchart, or overhead transparency, to establish the fact that even though a culture may be narcissistic, individual characters within it may exhibit one or more of Wilson's (1993) moral sentiments. For example, one student exhibited empathy when she intervened, quieting the class, when the novice teacher, LouAnn Johnson, could not.

Tuesday through Thursday. Using Bambara's "A Girl's Story" and Chopin's "The Story of an Hour," continue to develop the identity theme focusing upon main characters, RaeAnn and Louise respectively. Put emphasis upon the tandems contained in Damon's moral system: self-understanding and social cognition; the moral sentiments and moral judgment.

A possible lesson scenario using "A Girl's Story" would focus upon RaeAnn's personal quest for identity, which is influenced by her innocence as well as her adolescent egocentrism. Her lack of knowledge and confusion stemming from normal teenage physical change serves as a metaphor for the confusion she feels about herself not only as a young woman but also as an African American. Using an interactive discussion, have students identify RaeAnn's internal conflicts as they relate to her physical development and her confusion dealing with her personal as well as collective identity (Woolfolk, 1998). In addition, have students elaborate upon RaeAnn's concerns dealing with identity issues as they relate to Damon's moral system, specifically the tandem of self-understanding and social cognition.

Unlike the teenage RaeAnn, who is at the identity vs. identity role confusion stage of her social development, the married woman, Louise Mallard in "The Story of an Hour," faces a different developmental crisis, intimacy vs. isolation, with the accidental death of her husband, Brently (Erikson, 1963). Using an interactive discussion raise the following question with students: Is Louise a good wife, or is she narcissistic, only thinking selfishly of her anticipated freedom? Does she value her personal freedom more than her spouse? Guide the reflective discussion (Kindsvatter et al., 1996) to help students develop their own moral systems by encouraging them to make ethical judgments regarding the nature or goodness of Louise's character.

Note-taking is a learning strategy that most secondary school students need to cultivate. Therefore, during this unit students are taught to use the "notes and quotes" approach (Burke, 1999, pp. 46–47). Students are instructed to divide notepaper into two sections. On the left side they select quotes or events they think are essential to the literary works themselves as well the unit's *identity* theme. On the right-hand of the notepaper they reflect on the meaning and importance of their selected quote(s). Students will use this approach throughout the unit as their major note-taking device. Periodically the teacher will review student work for feedback and accountability. In addition, students will have the option to use the accumulated "notes and quotes" as the basis for a major project at the unit's end.

Friday. Looking back as well as looking forward, use a comparison-contrast cognitive map (Hyerle, 1996) on a flipchart to focus upon LouAnne and students from *Dangerous Minds* and characters from the "The Story of an Hour" and "A Girl's Story." Highlight issues of self-understanding and social cognition (identity) as segues to *Hamlet.* For homework, assign students to identify at least one famous quote. For example, the teacher can cite the famous "To be or not to be" soliloquy. Then have each student take her selected quote and transfer it to an index card, which will facetiously be used as "a permission slip for admittance" to the next day's class.

Week Two

Monday. After collecting students' entrance slips, call upon student volunteers to discuss their selected quotes, then record them onto a class chart (poster board, flipchart, or bulletin board will do). Post the chart for the length of the unit; it will serve to cue prior knowledge as well as generate discussion. As the play unfolds, each quote should be highlighted (e.g., with a colored fluorescent marker) in order to recognize and reinforce student contributions. Use K, What Do I Know?, and W, What Do I Want to Find Out?, from the K-W-L+ (Ogle, 1989) strategy to introduce *Hamlet* by putting students in small collaborative groups. Instruct students to brainstorm and record what they know and what they want to know about *Hamlet* onto inexpensive write-on overhead transparencies. For homework, assign students to read Act I, scenes 1 and 2. The teacher's homework is to collate and nutshell each group's information regarding what they know (K) and what they want to know (W) into cogent visuals using write-on transparencies or, better yet, using computer software programs such as *Inspiration* (1998) or Microsoft's *PowerPoint* (1995).

Tuesday. At the lesson's entry present the nutshelled small-group work culled from the previous class (see Figure 5.1 and 5.2). Then, using a large-scale map and/or electronic resource such as *Encarta: Virtual Globe 99* (1993–98) or *Cartopedia: The Ultimate World Reference Atlas* (1995), ensure that students can more readily recognize and comprehend the geopolitical importance of Denmark, Poland, Norway, and England. Through interactive recitation (Kindsvatter et al., 1996), query the students regarding the drama's central plot, characters, and settings, while concurrently connecting elements of the moral system discussed last week

Figure 5.1 "K" Adapted from Ogle's K-W-L+ Approach

to Act I, scenes 1 and 2. As a graphic reminder for the class, record the aforementioned information on the third element (L) of the K-W-L+ strategy (see Figure 5.3). This ongoing, developmental class chart should be displayed prominently in the classroom. For homework, have students read Act I, scene 3.

Wednesday. As class begins, play the 1988 CD selection of Harry Chapin's song, "Cat's in the Cradle." Have students listen and read lyrics simultaneously, then tell them that today's lesson deals with family relationships, in particular fathers and sons, as well as brothers and sisters. Have students read silently Polonius's advice to Laertes, Act I, scene 3, lines 58 to 81 to identify what Polonius values. Cue and then play the videotape of Branagh and Ritstein's version of *Hamlet* (1996), viewing this same scene. Following the clip, initiate an interactive discussion using the following questions as a guide: What kind of a father is Polonius? Is he

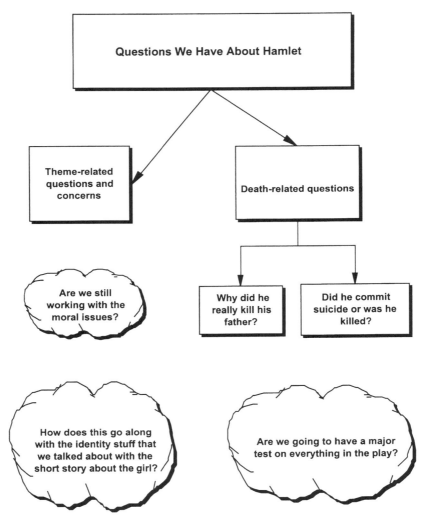

Figure 5.2 "W" Adapted from K-W-L+ Format

someone to be reckoned with and feared, or listened to and admired? How does Laertes react to his father's advice? Does Laertes take him seriously? Why? Why not? Does Polonius have his son's best interests in mind? Would *you* follow Polonius's advice? Since families generally provide the central support for developing personal values (social cognition and moral judgment) and in discovering who we are (self-understanding),

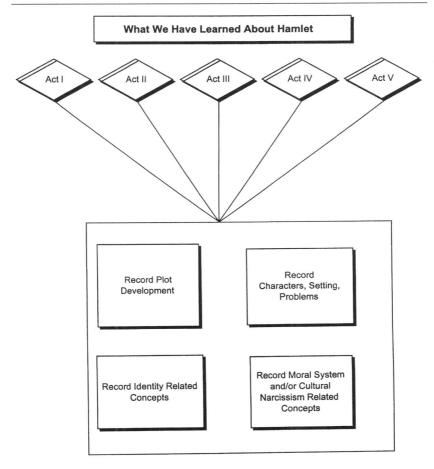

Figure 5.3 "L" Adapted from K-W-L+ Format. Complete chart during class as a way to reinforce plot and thematic issues.

highlight Polonius's sense of duty to provide his son with advice that will guide him socially and help him to make sound moral judgments. Then extend the discussion of parent/child interpersonal dynamics to sibling relationships by focusing upon Laertes' concern (empathy) for his sister, Ophelia. For homework, read Act I, scenes 4 and 5, reminding students to keep track of their "notes and quotes" responsibilities.

Thursday. Begin class with a brief 5-minute identification quiz to ensure that students have been keeping up with the reading, followed by a 15-minute period for an analytic, open book, essay question which focuses upon character development and at least one aspect of the moral system. For example, using textual evidence from Act I, support whether or not one of the characters is a moral decision-maker. Character choices include Claudius, Polonius, Laertes, Gertrude, Ophelia, Hamlet, and Hamlet's father (Ghost). Following the quiz, introduce concepts of trust and empathy among friends, Horatio and Hamlet, versus fairness and duty to fathers as presented by Hamlet and his father. Relate this to adolescent issues of loyalty and empathy among peers versus duty towards parents. For homework, read Act II, scenes 1 and 2.

Friday. Tape and use an introductory or lead promotional segment from a popular syndicated talk radio program such as the "Dr. Laura" (Schlessinger) show to cue students that they will be discussing moral dilemmas. Problem-solving scenario: You have a close friend who is exhibiting a threatening behavior, for example, excessive alcohol abuse, promiscuous sexual activity, or intravenous drug use. You have tried to counsel your friend confidentially, but to no avail. You are worried that your friend's health and welfare may be in jeopardy. Moral dilemma: Do you tell your friend's family members? What would you do?

Have students find classmates who support or share their opinions (multiple perspective-taking). This may necessitate the formation of several groups of like-minded students. Each group should provide a rationale for its decision which is shared with the class as a whole. Connect the student responses to a discussion of yesterday's in-class essay and today's examination of Ophelia's duty to her father and Polonius's responsibility to his king. For homework, have students read Act II, scene 3.

Week Three

Monday. Discuss the plot of Act II, scene 3 which students read for homework. Emphasize new characters and emerging conflicts while simultaneously updating the class' K-W-L+ chart (see Figure 5.3). Rosencrantz and Guildenstern, for example, are introduced as pawns of the king to figure out why Hamlet is so despondent. Continue to highlight issues related to the unit's central theme of identity as well as the moral sense, such as Rosencranz and Guildenstern's duty to the king versus the duty to their friend Hamlet. Again, remind students to maintain their "notes and quotes" responsibilities.

Tuesday. Television shows such as Fox's *Ally McBeal* make use of contemporary soliloquies. Spontaneously, videotape an episode or two from this (or other socially appropriate television broadcasts) looking for such soliloquies, then bring one or two to class to use as a very brief entry for today's lesson. Define *soliloquy* and discuss how it is conventionally used not only in Shakespearean works, but also in contemporary print (e.g., interior monologues found in "The Story of an Hour") and nonprint literature. Next, in order to develop further the identity theme, show a 3-minute excerpt from the *Hamlet* video beginning with Act II, scene 2: "O, what a rogue and peasant slave am I! / Is it not monstrous that this player here. . . ." Here Hamlet clearly reflects upon his cowardice and questions his own inability to respond to his father's demand for revenge. Pose the following questions to students: Is Hamlet, for example, a rational or emotional human being? Introduce the concept of Hamlet's sense of duty to his dead father and concept of fairness. Does he believe the ghost? Discuss.

Close class discussion, distribute unit projects (see Suggested Projects at the end of this unit), and then allow 15 to 20 minutes in order to answer student questions regarding them. Finally, give students tonight's homework assignment: read Act III, scene 1.

Wednesday. The purposes of today's class are to make sure that students recognize and understand the central conflicts of the play, and relate those conflicts to the four moral sentiments as a way of comprehending better the nature of conflict itself. First, review with the class four generic models of conflict found in virtually any drama: character vs. character, character vs. society, character vs. nature, and character vs. self. If needed, use a "think aloud," a metacognitive process whereby one not merely explains to the class examples and nonexamples of each type of conflict, but equally important shares one's thought processes, elaborating upon how one arrives at such categorization. For instance, one might highlight the character vs. himself as a central conflict—namely Hamlet's moral dilemma of whether or not to kill his stepfather. Does Hamlet sympathize with Claudius? To whom does Hamlet owe allegiance (duty), his new or deceased father (fairness)? Does Hamlet suppress his anger now, or act upon it later (self-control)? Put students into small collaborative groups so that they can generate their own examples of conflict within the play and have them connect the conflicts to one or more of the moral sentiments. Be sure to provide each group with a handout (see Figure 5.4) on which to record their responses for reporting back to the class as a whole.

To provide closure to today's lesson, boot the *Shakespeare Interactive* CD-ROM (1996), having students listen to a professional actor's oral interpretation of Hamlet's renowned "To be or not to be" soliloquy in order to not only highlight his internal ethical struggle, but also foster an

Conflict Day

Choose three of the following scenarios to address.

<table>
<tr>
<td valign="top">

Conflict Scenario 1: Character vs. Self

Who?
When?
Where?
Evidence of conflict?
How could conflict be resolved? Why?
What other options does the character have?
How do the character's actions relate to any one or more the following:

- Duty
- Empathy
- Fairness
- Self-control
- Sense of identity

</td>
<td valign="top">

Conflict Scenario 2: Character vs. Character

Who?
When?
Where?
Evidence of conflict?
How could conflict be resolved? Why?
What other options do the characters have?
How do the characters' actions relate to any one or more the following:

- Duty
- Empathy
- Fairness
- Self-control
- Sense of identity

</td>
</tr>
<tr>
<td valign="top">

Conflict Scenario 3: Character vs. Nature

Who?
When?
Where?
Evidence of conflict?
How could conflict be resolved? Why?
What other options does the character have?
How do the character's actions relate to any one or more the following:

- Duty
- Empathy
- Fairness
- Self-control
- Sense of identity

</td>
<td valign="top">

Conflict Scenario 4: Character vs. Society

Who?
When?
Where?
Evidence of conflict?
How could conflict be resolved? Why?
What other options does the character have?
How do the character's actions relate to any one or more the following:

- Duty
- Empathy
- Fairness
- Self-control
- Sense of identity

</td>
</tr>
</table>

Figure 5.4 Class handout for recognition of various types of character conflict.

aesthetic appreciation for the sound of the Bard's language. For home-work, students read Act III, scene 2.

Thursday. Since students may have difficulty conceptualizing "The Mousetrap," the play within the play (Act III, scene 2, lines 146 to 255), as a device "to catch the conscience of the king," use a video clip of this scene to help students envision the conflict taking place between Claudius and Hamlet as well to analyze each character's salient traits. Then pose questions such as, Are Hamlet and Claudius intelligent? What evidence is there to support your opinion? (If necessary, provide students with clues. For example, Hamlet was at the very least well educated, as he was able to recall and recite specific quotes from plays he had previously read.) What types of intelligences are portrayed by the different characters? What do their intelligence *profiles* (D'Arcangelo, 1997) suggest about their sense of identity as well as their moral judgment? Provide a capsule overview of Gardner's multiple intelligence theory with handout (Armstrong, 1994) to guide students for the discussion. Either consult readily available resources on the Internet using any one of a number of search engines, or review D'Arcangelo's CD-ROM entitled *Exploring Our Multiple Intelligences* (1997). Time permitting, have students form small groups to compare and contrast one another's responses. For homework, students read Act III, scene 3. Again, remind students to keep track of their "notes and quotes" responsibilities.

Friday. Put Damon's four-component moral system (1995) on the chalkboard. As today's lesson develops, listen especially carefully to individual student responses in order to record, reinforce, and visually connect their insights to one or more components of the moral system. During the first half of class, have students view and reflect upon at least one example of Elizabethan art that depicts a relationship between children and parents, such as Johnson's 1641 painting entitled *Arthur Capel, 1ˢᵗ Baron Capel, and his Family* (available at <http://www.english.upenn.edu/˜bushnell/english-30/materials/new_family/ >). Then, engage students in an interactive lecture reviewing Hamlet's relationships with Gertrude, Hamlet (ghost), and stepfather, Claudius. After this, have students compare and contrast these relationships with those of Ophelia, Laertes, and their father, Polonius. Finally, have students offer their opinions as to whether or not contemporary parent-child relationships have changed radically since Hamlet's day, centering on the two cultures' (i.e., both past and present) possible influences on family moral (read *value*) systems.

During the second half of class, focus upon Claudius's self-reflections, Act III, scene 3, lines 36 to 72, to refine further the class's understanding of the moral system. For example, in lines 36 to 38 ("O, my offense is rank, it smells to heaven; / It hath the primal eldest curse upon't,— / A brother's murder!"), identify and explain how Claudius's comments reflect his self-understanding, social cognition, and moral judgment. Then prompt students to reread carefully Claudius's soliloquy to discover additional contextual evidence of his moral system.

Conclude the lesson by reviewing student contributions noted on the chalkboard. Then conduct a written exit poll asking students the following questions: Will Hamlet kill Claudius and Gertrude? Why? Why not? What are his motivations?

Week Four

Monday. First, show the video clip of Act III, scene 4, lines 1 through 103, which depicts Hamlet's accidental assassination of Polonius and the verbal confrontation and advisement with Gertrude, his mother. Drawing upon this video segment, as well as the data gleaned from last class's exit poll, lead an interactive discussion posing questions where needed such as: Does Hamlet in any way display love or affection for his mother? Is he empathetic or just? When he kills Polonius, does Hamlet display any remorse for his actions? Why or why not? What does his behavior suggest regarding his level or ability to empathize with others, or to control his actions when confused? Encourage students to draw inferences about taking responsibility (read *duty*) for one's own actions as well as seeing the world through another's eyes (read *social cognition*). For example, isn't Gertrude, Hamlet's mother, at least partially responsible for his rash actions and erratic disposition because of her hasty marriage to Claudius? In the beginning of this scene, Gertrude does not take such responsibility (in lines 40–41 she says, "What have I done that thou dar'st wag thy tongue / In noise so rude against me?"). However, within a very brief period of time, she does acknowledge her culpability (lines 89–92: "O Hamlet, speak no more. / Thou turn'st mine eyes into my very soul, / And there I see such black and grained spots / As will not leave their tint.").

In the closing moments of today's lesson, have students speculate about Hamlet's willingness to murder again. For example, having once committed homicide, will he no longer agonize over assassinating Claudius?

Tuesday. If appropriate, graphically recap plot elements of the play using the "L" of the class K-W-L+ chart. Elements, at this juncture, might include the king's growing fear of Hamlet with his concomitant wish to banish and kill him using Rosencrantz and Guildenstern as accomplices, Hamlet's journey to England, and Fortenbras's progress with his armies (Act IV, scenes 1 to 4). To foreshadow Wednesday's class, show the video clip cued to the scene which dramatizes Ophelia's death.

Provide about 15 to 20 minutes of class time to clarify student project choices, making sure to emphasize the time-line for project completion. For homework, students read Act IV, scenes 5 through 7.

Wednesday. Using Hamlet's "To be or not to be" soliloquy, reframed as to be or not to be a moral person, begin class today by displaying a photograph of "Judge Judy" or former Mayor Koch while asking students to recount how the popular TV show, *The People's Court*, operates. After they respond, pose the following questions: Is Hamlet a moral person? Is Laertes a moral person? Extend to Claudius. When the brief discussion ends, divide the class into small groups of four or five students apiece. Assign each group the responsibility to either defend or prosecute Hamlet, Laertes, Gertrude, or Claudius based upon evidence of each one's moral character. Provide write-on transparencies and erasable markers to small groups so that each one can identify their character, make moral judgments about their character, and provide contextual support for their defense or prosecution. Students present their evidence to the teacher and rest of the class, as the teacher assumes the role of the presiding judge in order to ascertain quality of evidence used to defend or accuse each character. Be sure to emphasize the similarities and differences between Laertes and Hamlet on their quest for revenge. In order to ensure that students have been keeping up with the reading, announce that there will be a brief objective quiz that will take place at the beginning of the tomorrow's class. For homework, students read Act V, scene 1.

Thursday. After administering today's quiz, begin class by playing a student-created (or teacher-created) audiotape that summarizes basic plot issues. Entitled "Conflict Update: In Castle Elsinore" this brief 60-second tape simulates a local news-radio report. News items include a bulletin on Fortenbras's army's progress and a feature report on Ophelia's burial. Or, as an alternative summary, use the Time Line "hotspot" feature on the *Shakespeare Interactive* CD-ROM (1996).

In order to understand and appreciate more fully Hamlet's identity confusion, show the video clip of Act V, scene 1 (lines 58 to 204). Discuss Hamlet's wit and sense of humor as evidenced by his banter with the gravedigger. Continue playing the tape, lines 205 to 285, in order to reveal his moral development by analyzing his actions at Ophelia's gravesite. For instance, ask students to note Hamlet's lack of self-control and absence of empathy for Laertes in his grief over his loss. For homework, read Act V, scenes 1 and 2. Again, remind students to keep track of their "notes and quotes" responsibilities.

Friday. The main purposes of today's lesson are to finish the reading and viewing of the play and to provide closure for unit's identity theme. Show the final video clip of the drama, Act V, scene 2, lines 214 to the end. Use the K-W-L+ chart to recap the final scene of *Hamlet*. Finally, conduct an interactive discussion focusing on the resolution of major plot conflicts as contained in *Hamlet*, "The Story of an Hour," and "A Girl's Story." Focus especially on the protagonists' words and deeds as they relate to identity and the moral system: self-understanding (self-identity. Who am I?), social cognition (self-discovery through interaction with others. How do I fit in?), moral sentiments (self-identity. What do I think and feel about myself and others?), and moral judgment (self-discovery. How do I evaluate the actions of myself as well as others?). For homework, students study for the unit test by reviewing their "notes and quotes," teacher handouts, and the class K-W-L+ chart.

Week Five
Monday. Administer the unit test. For homework, students work on their projects (delineated below).

Tuesday through Wednesday. Provide opportunity for students to have miniconferences to clarify issues regarding their projects. Workshops begin: Students are provided opportunities to prepare and work on their capstone projects.

Thursday through Friday. Project presentations are shared.

Suggested Projects: Quest for Identity Unit

Using a creative blending of both idea and product technologies, the following projects are designed to give students opportunities to show, in their own ways, what they have learned. Each option with its underlying technologies is described briefly. When students are encouraged to use a variety of idea and product technologies, their imaginations may be fueled and their various intelligences ignited. Teachers should make their own modifications and accommodations in order to meet individual student and unique classroom needs. Although the following projects focus on *Hamlet*, teachers should consider adapting these ideas to extend to and include the other unit literary works.

Option #1: Multimedia Presentation
Using either *PowerPoint* (1995) or *HyperStudio* (1993–98), students create and demonstrate a multimedia presentation which is based upon their accumulated "notes and quotes." The goal of this project presentation is to show how specific characters in the literary works that they studied have dealt with identity issues related to making moral judgments. For example, one student may contend that Ophelia's death was a deliberate suicide, whereas another may view her demise as the end result of a mental breakdown. In order to provide textual evidence to support their theses, students need to incorporate their "notes and quotes" in their

presentations. In addition, students are encouraged to download pictures, graphics, audio files, and so on. from any one of a number of web sites devoted to "The Bard," or may choose to compose their own images using a digital camera. The following web addresses (a.k.a. uniform resource locators or URLs) may be used as springboards for their investigations:

- http://www.rdg.ac.uk/AcaDepts/In/Globe/home.html
- http://www-tech.mit.edu/Shakespeare/Quotes/bart.Hamlet.html
- http://us.imdb.com/Tsearch?title=hamlet&restrict=Movies+and+ TV&submit4.x=10&submit4.x=10&submit4.y=9
- http://www.ulen.com/shakespeare/teachers/lessons/
- http://www.shakespearemag.com/fall96/hamlet.asp
- http://www.sdcoe.k12.ca.us/score/ham/hamtg.html
- http://www.people.virginia.edu/~dlf3m/bardquest/bardquest.html
- http://henson.austin.apple.com/edres/shlessons/sh-lithamlet.shtml
- http://www.shakespeare.com
- http://www.cs.ushd.edu.au/~matty/c

The Internet and World Wide Web are constantly evolving; thus, teachers should review all sites listed in this book for accuracy and appropriateness before using them in the classroom.

Option #2: Lethal Weapon
Could Hamlet have resolved his conflicts with Gertrude, Claudius, and Laertes without resorting to the use of violence and lethal weaponry? Compare the protagonist, Riggs, in the film *Lethal Weapon* to the protagonist in Gibson's laserdisc version of *Hamlet* (Lovell, 1990). Does Hamlet, like Riggs, employ excessive use of force? Does Hamlet have other options? Have students investigate these three questions using the four components of the moral system as a basic framework. For example, in the soliloquy in Act I, scene 2, lines 129 to 159, Hamlet recounts his anger regarding his father's death and his mother's hasty remarriage. Indicate that this might have been a timely opportunity for Hamlet to have empathized (a moral sentiment) with Gertrude, by viewing the situation through *her* eyes, trying to understand *her* decision to remarry (social cognition and perspective-taking). Student oral presentations should be accompanied by the laserdisc version of Gibson's *Hamlet* to illustrate specific opportunities where the protagonist could or should have exercised more self-control. Note: the laserdisc has instant random

access capabilities: no need for time-consuming fast-forwarding or rewinding.

Option #3: I'm Listening

Have students simulate a call-in talk radio show entitled, "I'm Listening," which is modeled on the popular television sitcom, *Frasier*. Students must invent questions and devise answers that reflect their understanding of the moral system as presented during the unit. Students will not only produce and write the script, but also solicit their classmates' help to participate as audience callers (even family members could be audiotaped). For example: If a call-in radio show existed during the Elizabethan Age, what questions would the characters in *Hamlet* ask the host, and what ethical advice would the host give? For example, how might Dr. Crane, the esteemed psychiatrist, advise Ophelia when she calls him crying about her boyfriend, Hamlet, who dumped her?

Option #4: Hamlet on Trial: A WebQuest

Use Bernie Dodge's WebQuest (1999), a six-part idea technology, to develop the following scenario. Hamlet is charged for the murders of Polonius, Claudius, and Leartes as well the reckless endangerment of his mother, Gertrude, and former girlfriend, Ophelia. You are his lawyer. What ethical and/or legal arguments could you use to defend your client? Prepare a legal brief and present your opening remarks to the court, commenting upon why you, as his lawyer, felt compelled to accept his case.

Option #5: Lethal Lampoon

Have students satirize six of *Hamlet's* major characters by creating a set of political cartoons, each one lampooning an individual character. Students will present their drawings and captions to the class, explicating the ethical or moral issues that underlie each lampoon.

Option #6: I Am Justly Killed with Mine Own Treachery

Have students compose, set to music, and perform a rap, song or lyric poem dealing with a specific moral dilemma that a character in the play had to address. For example, in Act V, scene 2, Hamlet and Laertes duel to their deaths. A group of students could choreograph and reenact this scene by composing a song or rap that dramatizes Laertes' moral dilemma: Is it fair for Laertes to duel Hamlet when he knows the weapon he holds is tipped with poison and Hamlet's is not? In the song Leartes might muse aloud how he, although enraged about his sister's death, struggles with the fact that the duel is heavily weighted in his favor.

Analysis/Discussion: Blending Idea and Product Technologies

It is challenging to isolate and discuss as separate entities the idea and product technologies employed in this unit plan in that they are often integrally blended in order to support each lesson's instructional emphasis. Damon's moral system, the predominant idea technology, provides the basic organizational framework for the unit, yet it is nevertheless enriched and amplified when conjoined with one or more additional idea and/or product technologies.

Dangerous Minds (Simpson & Bruckheimer, 1995), the video-based entry to the first lesson, provides not only a motivational mindset, but also a contemporary example of how the moral system can be addressed. In this lesson the entry suggests that empathy can indeed exist within a culture replete with self-absorption. As the unit unfolds, other lesson entries again blend the moral system with a variety of product and idea technologies in order to activate student prior knowledge, introduce new concepts, and create fresh perspectives for the class to draw upon when analyzing the literary works. The "Cat's in the Cradle" lyric (Chapin, 1988), for instance, encourages students to relate to and identify with an important family issue embedded in contemporary parent/child relationships as a prelude to analyzing and understanding Hamlet's interactions with his deceased father and conniving stepfather. While this set induction uses a modern musical piece to cue students to the ongoing difficulties that adolescents presently face, it also helps them to recognize the timeless and universal nature of moral decision making. Each of the set inductions described above foreshadows intentional learning where students reflect upon the actions of the characters.

Instructional activities require students to respond to the work's ethical conflicts by analyzing, synthesizing, or evaluating characters' actions using contextual evidence. Student responses may incorporate various forms of product technology such as overhead transparencies, flip charts, computer presentations, and so on. Questions posed in the lessons reflect Kindsvatter et al.'s questioning levels (1996), which provide a systematic format to structure critical thinking opportunities. When the learners, either independently or in small groups, reflect upon the motivations of characters' actions, they, in turn, have opportunities to reflect upon their own actions and decision-making skills. It is these opportunities that promote student self-understanding, social cognition, moral reasoning and judgment as well as opportunities that suggest alternative responses to the prevailing and possibly narcissistic cultural norms.

Another instructional activity demonstrates how Gardner's multiple intelligence theory complements Damon's moral system. The activity in which students are introduced to a rudimentary outline of Gardner's multiple intelligence theory addresses several concurrent purposes. Character analysis and motivation are important structural concerns when teaching any literary work. In using the multiple intelligence activity, students formulate character sketches of the main players while simultaneously developing basic understandings of how individual differences can impact one's decision-making skills—their own as well as Hamlet's. Using reflective, interactive questioning techniques (Kindsvatter et al., 1996) the teacher helps the students view the characters through the specific lens of multiple intelligence theory and recognize how individuals interact with their emotional and physical environments in unique ways. This activity may lead students to raise basic questions of self, and provide them with opportunities to reflect upon their individual intelligence profiles as they relate to all four elements of the moral system: self-understanding, social cognition, moral sentiments, and moral judgment.

As stated in the beginning of this chapter, teachers face curricular demands that Burke (1999) suggests are rife with opportunities that encourage conversation regarding moral issues. But in order to engage in intellectually meaningful and productive discourse *in an English Language Arts classroom*, students' collective knowledge and attention should be directed toward the literary work itself. Unfortunately, some literary works, especially those as complex and beautifully poetic as Shakespeare's *Hamlet*, can pose formidable challenges for adolescents. Sometimes, for instance, students seemingly fail to understand basic plot and conflict developments because of syntactical sophistication and novel vocabulary. At other times students, because of reading disabilities, absenteeism, or lethargy, encounter difficulty assimilating not only the rudimentary who, what, when, and where facts, but also the whys and hows dealing with higher level thematic and moral issues. Ogle's (1989) K-W-L+ provides a systematic approach that promotes learner engagement by activating prior knowledge, establishing purposes for learning, monitoring newly acquired information, and connecting prior with new information to form a cohesive personal statement (the "+" aspect of the K-W-L+ idea technology). When adapted for a secondary classroom, K-W-L+ serves not only reluctant readers who require structure but also spatial learners who need to visualize character, plot, and setting—those adolescents who need to see physically the basics before more fully comprehending and appreciating theme.

Responding to text in a personal manner helps students to engage intimately with a work's central issues as well as improve their critical reading strategies (Burke, 1999; Rosenblatt, 1968). "Notes and quotes" presents a systematic approach in engaging students to construct personal meaning as well as to reflect upon identity and moral system elements presented in the unit's literary works. When teachers present "notes and quotes," a form of reader response whereby students reflect upon and critique the notes that they have written based upon their unfolding awareness of one or more elements of the moral system, it serves as an idea technology rather than a simplistic note-taking mechanism.

Many of the idea technologies included in this unit serve dual purposes, both as instructional supports and as assessment tools that provide teachers with routine yet vital student feedback. For example, the "notes and quotes" strategy provides students with targeted quotes and reflections that learners can readily refer to during class discussions. Additionally, "notes and quotes" serve as student study guides for quizzes as well as the unit test and capstone project.

Not only an instructional tool, the class K-W-L+ chart serves as an informal formative assessment barometer of students' reading comprehension. Critical to the K-W-L+ strategy is its fourth component, the "+," wherein learners are encouraged to synthesize prior with newly acquired knowledge. The capstone unit projects function as formal "+" components for the K-W-L+ developed during the *Hamlet* phase of the unit. Each project requires students to demonstrate what they have learned about the literary content, albeit with an ethical emphasis and with encouragement to use product technology to complement their new knowledge.

The proposed unit projects assess both students' content mastery as well as their understanding of various components of the moral system. Although each project is unique in its design and requirements, all are grounded in the subject matter content and crafted to promote student processing of the moral system in relation to some aspect of the literary work. In addition, the projects are intended to engender student reflection of their own moral system, moral decision making, and self-understanding as they investigate the ethical issues inherent in each project.

In order to provide students with robust opportunities to demonstrate what they have learned, the six aforementioned project options reflect a conscious decision to adapt Gardner's multiple intelligence theory, an idea technology, to the secondary English language arts classroom. All projects possess an appropriate linguistic requirement, yet each encourages students to draw upon other intellectual talents as well. For example, option #3, I'm Listening, may not only entice students who possess strong interpersonal skills, but also those who wish to cultivate and share reflective intrapersonal insights. Wouldn't adolescent peers be captivated by talk show hosts who are adept at responding sensitively, perhaps humorously, to the audience callers?

The multimedia presentation (option #1) with its emphasis on educational technology prompts students to use their "notes and quotes" to showcase characters' struggles with moral judgments. In order to complete such an assignment, students need to delve more deeply into a single fictional character and examine particular instances of his or her moral decision making. Such analyses promote student self-reflection, as adolescents use their own experiences as baselines. Exploring the similarities and differences between a fictional character's ethical choices and those of a contemporary teenager creates a challenging yet provocative learning context, one that cultivates personal reflection and fosters greater self-awareness as students grapple with personal and social conflicts, the foundation of all human drama. When students extend their investigations further to include web site reviews and critiques, they may need to reconcile these new, external perspectives with their own when making determinations regarding a character's ethical or moral stance (social cognition). Choices of accompanying music, graphics, illustrations, and works of art, whether Elizabethan, Victorian, or modern, reflect not only the degree to which students wrestle with the moral dilemmas that emanate from their analytic investigations, but also indicates the amount of time, effort, and care students take in preparing for their PowerPoint or HyperStudio presentation.

Excessive use of force is a common topical issue in both our nation's electronic and print news media. Like a dead metaphor or pair of brown socks, excessive force has become so culturally pervasive that it has been rendered lifeless or invisible; thus, many citizens, let alone impressionable adolescents, no longer contemplate the meanings and implications of the words and images contained in our daily news reports. With this in mind, the *Lethal Weapon* project (option #2) propels students into an investigation of Hamlet's use of verbal abuse or physical violence as his primary tools for resolving personal problems. The video of *Lethal Weapon* establishes a motivational backdrop that reinforces universal, moral decision-making issues that face the historical and modern protagonists, Hamlet and Riggs, respectively. The four components of the moral system serve as guideposts for students to use when examining Hamlet's conflicts and responses, when generating alternative resolutions to his moral dilemmas, and when drawing comparisons and contrasts between Elizabethan and contemporary society. Questions students generate regarding Hamlet's actions and moral choices may mirror questions and concerns about their own use of excessive force, whether verbal or physical.

I'm Listening, option #3, addresses both tandems of the moral system. For example, as student hosts listen to characters and provide solutions to their dilemmas, learners cultivate their perspective-taking abilities by considering problems from others' points of view, and reflect upon those views as fictional "therapists" (social cognition and self-understanding). To help the call-in clients, student hosts must differentiate between personal responses with the needs of the callers in mind. In so doing hosts *first* invoke and *then* apply empathy and fairness as they consider all of the mitigating circumstances revealed in the play (moral sentiments and moral judgment). Students who role-play the characters who call in are required to understand their individual character's motivation, personality, and internal conflicts. This enables them to develop questions that move from mere low-order convergent to high-order divergent (Kindsvatter et al., 1996), thus blending Damon's moral system with another idea technology, a powerful questioning technique, which will help learners to develop content mastery as well as character.

For project option #4, preparing a legal brief for Hamlet's defense, Hamlet on Trial: A WebQuest, students are encouraged to apply "high end states": those thinking and decision-making skills associated with individuals who have reached the pinnacle of the profession (Armstrong, 1994, pp. 5–6). To complete this project successfully students must surf the web using a systematic, teacher-created WebQuest protocol (Dodge, 1995) that prompts students to locate and analyze, as well as accept or reject information that could advance the case of their client. Inherent in this project are the ethical decisions that any trial lawyer must make when deciding *how* to defend or, perhaps more importantly, *whether* to defend an individual whose actions reflect a value system that may be contrary to their own.

Lethal Lampoon and I Am Justly Killed with Mine Own Treachery, project options #5 and #6, differ significantly from the first four. In Lethal Lampoon students must *satirize pictorially* each of *Hamlet's* major characters based upon their personal analysis of the characters' moral reasoning and moral judgments. Of equal value to the actual cartoon drawings are the captions and accompanying oral explications of the underlying moral issues depicted. As do the other projects, option #5 requires that students understand the characters' major conflicts, motivations, and behaviors in order to satirize their predicaments convincingly with appropriate wit and cunning. Project #6 also provides an opportunity for students to self-select a character who confronts a specific moral dilemma. But in this instance students create their own products *musically* to demonstrate their comprehension of the subtle moral issues involved.

Conclusion

This unit encourages students to explore the moral system as it is revealed within a selection of literature that is found in many secondary English language arts curricula. Such explorations may lead students to question their own belief systems and moral decision-making strategies. In some cases it may also encourage students to adopt concepts such as fairness, empathy, self-control, and duty as the basis for making personal decisions. Rather than targeting cultural narcissism explicitly, the Search for Identity unit addresses the following implicit instructional goals: to promote student mastery of content; to foster student awareness of the different elements of the moral system; and to help students recognize moral signposts by blending product and idea technologies which, in turn, enhance teaching and learning. This blend of technologies enables students to understand how the moral system can help them make more effective moral decisions. Specifically, the set inductions, activities, discussions, and assessment instruments provide students with a range of opportunities to muse and personally question what they value and how they either do or do not recognize and respond to moral challenges presented to them in their culture. These opportunities constitute an initial step in addressing many of the narcissistic manifestations present in our culture.

Chapter Six

Character Education in the Social Studies Classroom

As explained in Chapter 1, character education has in various forms been a constant component of the educational enterprise since colonial times. While character education was often done as part of history instruction during the nineteenth-century, it appeared regularly during the first half of the twentieth-century in a wide range of activities in the social studies classroom. However, responding to national and international events, the primacy of the social studies as the centerpiece of character education diminished from the 1960s through the 1970s (McClellan, 1992).

With the launching of the Russian satellite *sputnik*, the United States was thrust into the space race. To compete with the Soviets, the federal government urged school districts to include more mathematics and science in the curriculum, often at the expense of the social studies (McClellan, 1992). Moreover, in the wake of the Vietnam War and the Watergate scandal, a tenor of cynicism towards the government as well as towards other traditional institutions, including the family and the school, resulted in questioning the very values on which such institutions were based. This cynicism was also accompanied by a national soul-searching that was spurred on by the Civil Rights Movement, a movement that revealed the hypocrisy surrounding the claim that all people were equally guaranteed life, liberty, and the pursuit of happiness.

Where social studies teachers continued to engage in character education, many were reluctant to discuss values or universal standards of conduct. This reluctance resulted not just from the cynical reactions to the social and political events of the 1960s and 1970s, but also from the increasing cultural and racial diversity that surfaced in so many public schools throughout the country, especially in urban schools. Many social

studies teachers believed that, at best, they should do no more than develop classroom activities that would lead students to confront and clarify
their own values. As discussed in chapter 1, the Values Clarification Movement seemed to serve the needs of the time, but as more conservative
critics pointed out, this approach did not necessarily guide students towards prosocial behavior. Reacting to the "contentlessness" (Sommers,
1984, p. 381) of values clarification, some teachers turned to more traditional and direct approaches to character education. But liberal critics of
these approaches stressed that such heavy-handed proselytizing would
restrain children's natural impulses and inquisitiveness, would not really
achieve their intended ultimate goals, and could conflict with the students'
and/or their parents' values and beliefs.

Recent research in social development provides promising implications
for doing character education in the classroom in a way that could medi-
ate the tension between these two approaches. As discussed in chapter 3,
Damon (1995) argued that a person's moral development continues
throughout one's life span and that this development is based on four
interpenetrating components: self-understanding, social cognition, moral
judgment, and the moral sense. With its emphasis on social phenomena,
social dynamics, and the individual's place within the social fabric, the
social studies has a rich potential for developing a student's self-understanding and social cognition (see chapter 3 for a full discussion of the
developmental interplay between these concepts). Likewise, the social
studies provide opportunities to raise questions of moral judgment in
historical and social contexts and, concomitantly, to engage students in
refining their moral judgment. The moral compass for such judgment
would proceed from the moral sentiments identified by Wilson (1993):
sympathy, fairness, duty, and self-control.

As explained in chapter 2, cultural narcissism is a powerful social force
that can undermine the development and functioning of the moral system. Many adolescents, and even preadolescents, exhibit in their classroom behavior the grandiosity, self-absorption, sense of entitlement, and
devaluation of others that are some of the more patent traits of cultural
narcissism. And where such traits are displayed by many youngsters, these
behaviors tend to become contagious, thus affecting those other adolescents who are especially vulnerable to peer influence.

Social studies teachers should find opportunities to refine all components of the moral system, while simultaneously combating the negative
forces of cultural narcissism. What follows are various models of instruction for social studies teachers that develop the moral system and con-

front cultural narcissism through a blending of idea and product technology (see chapter 4 for a detailed account of these technologies). These instructional models will focus on teaching nineteenth-century American social history, geography, and historical biography. While each model spans several days of instruction, each may be modified in length to address the needs of individual teachers. This section will conclude with a full-unit model of instruction on "Immigration, Multiculturalism, and Identity."

American Social History, Gender, and the Visual Arts

The teaching of American social history presents numerous opportunities for students to explore the role of females and family life in American culture. Such analysis also provides female students a baseline for further analysis of their own self-understanding as well as their understanding of other females as well as males. It provides a similar baseline for male students to examine their own self-understanding and to refine their social cognition.

American history texts frequently provide historical interpretations of the role of females, with some texts even providing brief biographies of women who have changed the course of history and influenced American life significantly. Other texts include primary documents central to female equality and suffrage, such as the Seneca Falls Resolution. Few texts, however, include the use of visuals that address the changing roles of women in American society. Heinich, Molenda, Russell, and Smaldino (1999) explained the benefits of using pictorials and graphics in reinforcing the mastery of core concepts. Gardner (1983, 1993) especially has argued for tapping into various intelligences when teaching, including spatial intelligence. Here, he commented that "the visual arts also employ this (spatial) intelligence in the use of space" (1993, p. 22).

Social studies teachers should consider supplementing their presentation of women in American history with the use of American portrait painting. Particularly effective are the paintings of Smibert, Feke and Copley. These paintings, which may also be viewed as product technologies, capture changes in family structure during the 18th and 19th centuries, especially as these reconfigurations reveal changes in the respective roles of females and children at that time in American society. In terms of the moral system, these paintings offer a context for nurturing student self-understanding and their social cognition, and they can be further used to develop moral judgment and to refine the moral sense.

Suggested Lesson Plan

Developing Self-Understanding and Social Cognition

1. Teacher shows slides of Feke's "Isaac Royal and Family" (1741) and Smibert's "Dean George Berkeley and his Family" (1729) side-by-side using two slide projectors [See Figures 6.1 and 6.2]. In groups, students discuss relationships between/among the male and female figures in the paintings.

2. Teacher shows slides of Copley's "Mr. and Mrs. Thomas Mifflin" (1773) and Copley's "The Copley Family" (1776) side-by-side on two projectors. [See Figures 6.3 and 6.4]. In groups, students discuss relationships between/among male and female figures in the paintings.

3. Teacher leads large-group discussion, synthesizing common observations from each group.

4. In groups, students sketch on paper the relative height of each male and each female character in the paintings.

5. In large-group discussion, the teacher emphasizes that males, particularly in the Feke and the Smibert, are spatially taller and more vertical than the females, who tend to be sitting, and that the males are often depicted with arms bent at the elbow or akimbo, a symbol of power and dominance. The discussion concentrates on how this reflects rank and position in society.

6. Teacher lectures on changing roles of females in American society between the Pre-revolutionary Period and the Civil War. Students read relevant sections from the text or from collateral handouts.

7. Student journal entries: Designed to foster self-understanding and social cognition, guiding questions for journal entries may be:

8. "Do the gender relationships in the paintings match my own understanding of my role as a female or male in contemporary American society, for example, in my family, in clubs I belong to, in school activities I participate in, in social groups I associate with?"

9. "Do I relate to the opposite gender in ways depicted by the characters in the paintings? Why or why not?"

10. Students collect clippings from magazines depicting gender relationships. In small groups, students compare/contrast the gender relationships in these photos to the gender relationships in the paintings. Students identify differences in these relationships and speculate on reasons for these changes, citing data from previous lecture and readings.

Figure 6.1 *Isaac Royal and family*, (1741) by Robert Feke. Courtesy of Art & Visual Materials, Special Collections Department, Harvard Law School Library.

Figure 6.2 John Smibert. *Dean Berkeley and His Entourage (The Bermuda Group).*(1731). Yale University Art Gallery. Gift of Isaac Lothrop.

Figure 6.3 John Singleton Copley. *Portrait of Mr. and Mrs. Thomas Mifflin (Sarah Morris)*, 1773. Philadelphia Museum of Art: Bequest of Mrs. Esther B. Wistar to the Historical Society of Pennsylvania in 1900, and acquried by the Philadelphia Museum of Art by mutual agreement with the Society through the great generosity of Mr. and Mrs. Fitz Eugene Dixon, Jr. and significant contributions from Mrs. Meyer Eglin and other donors, as well as the George W. Elkins Fund and the W.P. Wilstach Fund..

Figure 6.4 John Singleton Copley, *The Copely Family*, Andrew W. Mellon Fund, © 1999 Board of Trustees, National Gallery of Art, Washington DC.

Applying the Full Moral System: Refining the Moral Sentiments and Moral Judgment

1. Teacher introduces Wilson's (1993) four moral sentiments on overhead transparency: sympathy, fairness, duty, and self-control. In small groups, students discuss how these sentiments are present in and absent from modern American life. Continuing in small groups, students examine how these four sentiments are reflected in the paintings.

2. For homework, students search for additional examples of family life in magazine photos and advertisements and on TV commercials. Possible journal entries may ask students to analyze how the emotions in these contemporary magazines are different from/similar to the emotions displayed in the paintings presented in class. Are they different from Wilson's? What might account for these differences/similarities?

3. In groups, students speculate on what the modern commercials and the earlier paintings might look like if one or some of Wilson's sentiments were removed. (For example, What might the figures be doing if duty or sympathy were not a motivating feature in the photo or painting?) Students could also role-play these scenes and/or capture these on video or on slide-film to be shown to the class later as part of a group project. Additional journal entries: students exercise moral judgments (based on violations of moral sentiments that are depicted in the paintings and/or photos) focusing on whether these are lapses in social propriety or true violations of morality.

Cultural Narcissism

1. Teacher introduces Lasch's (1979) concept of cultural narcissism, using overhead transparencies and handouts with characteristics of narcissism.

2. In small groups, students discuss the validity of Lasch's thesis and the prevalence of cultural narcissism in their own lives.

3. For homework, students search magazine ads and TV commercials that reveal elements of cultural narcissism. Journal entries emphasize student analysis of these photos and/or TV commercials. For example, they would examine how narcissism might compromise the development of prosocial behavior (sharing, cooperating, helping, etc.).

4. Students share their journal entries, examining how cultural narcissism can thwart the development of prosocial behavior.

5. Closure via full-class interactive discussion on narcissism, prosocial behavior, and moral conduct. Suggested questions could include: How can cultural narcissism interfere with prosocial behavior? Is prosocial behavior the bedrock of moral conduct? Is prosocial behavior in some contexts influenced by gender stereotypes? Is such prosocial behavior and gender stereotypes captured in students' magazine clippings? In the paintings?

Analysis and Discussion: Blending Idea and Product Technologies

The above activities illustrate the use of idea and product technologies as partners in creating learning environments that enhance instruction, reinforce content mastery, and foster character education. As explained in chapter 4, an idea technology is a cognitive schema or blueprint designed to explain and guide a practice. In these activities, Gardner's (1983) multiple intelligence theory, Bloom's cognitive taxonomy (Woolfolk, 1998), Piaget's cognitive stage theory (Piaget & Inhelder, 1969), and Damon's (1995) moral system act synergistically as idea technologies in guiding instruction and in raising prosocial and moral awareness. A product technology, which is tangible, includes high-tech and low-tech hardware and software. In these activities, the portrait paintings exemplify product technologies, although photos and other graphics and magazine clippings would also qualify.

Gardner's spatial intelligence is emphasized at various points of instruction, calling for students to engage their visual skills by clipping photos, by drawing, and by examining paintings. Student interpersonal skills, intrapersonal talents, and linguistic intelligence are respectively appealed to as they participate in group activities, journal writing, and note-taking. Bloom's cognitive paradigm guides teachers in developing activities that foster analysis as well as application and evaluation. Piaget's formal operational thought is reflected in student engagement in higher-order thinking, especially propositional and hypothetical thought.

As discussed in chapter 4, idea technologies are systemic in that elements *within* the idea can influence each other. Similarly, components of idea technologies can cross-fertilize components of other idea technologies. For instance, as students participate in Bloom-driven evaluation of what characters in the paintings might be doing if they were not motivated by moral sentiments, students are also reflecting Piaget's construct of formal operational, propositional thought as well as Damon's moral system.

The cross-fertilizing features of idea technologies are also exhibited *between* idea technologies and product technologies. In the above activities, the paintings are product technologies, whose *ideas* about life, gender, and society (the idea technology) germinated recursively in the respective minds of the painters as they captured these ideas on tangible canvas. As students gain familiarity with viewing paintings as depictions of gender and social arrangements, they gain confidence in transferring this analytical capacity to other visuals, such as magazine photos and TV commercials. Equally important, as students use Damon's moral system (an idea technology) to examine these visuals (product technologies), they should develop a deeper understanding of the visuals themselves. Simultaneously, this should lead to students developing those habits of mind that would heighten their sensitivity to their own prosocial behavior and lead to greater moral awareness.

Geography

There exists strong potential for engaging in character education in both economics and American government classrooms. Each discipline provides teachers countless opportunities to examine with their students the moral imperatives inherent in a broad range of issues, including national and regional spending policies, taxation, and equal representation before the law. American government classes additionally provide contexts for students to engage in role-playing and simulations that can directly thrust them into the legal process, a strategy used by many schools to teach principles of American law while simultaneously teaching character education. Perhaps the most popular of these approaches is law-related education, which is used in hundreds of high schools throughout the country. (See <http://clre.org> for additional information.)

Realistically, if a school district decided to implement the suggestions below (generating moral awareness by tapping into the moral sentiments while simultaneously countervailing the impact of cultural narcissism) such endeavors would most probably not be followed in all social studies classrooms, and certainly not in *both* economics and American government. If a teacher or curriculum supervisor had to choose just one social studies course to emphasize the moral sentiments and to reveal the potentially pejorative effects of cultural narcissism, it most probably should be geography. As Dewey noted in *The School and Society* (1899/1976):

> the unity of all the sciences is found in geography. The significance of geography is that it presents the earth as the enduring home of the occupations of man. The world without its relationship to human activity is less than a world. . . . [The

earth] is his continual shelter and protection, the raw material of all his activities, and the home to whose humanizing and idealizing all his achievements returns. (p. 13)

Placing these thoughts in a moral context, Smith (1995), a geographer at the University of London, pointed out that geography

> touches on a wide range of issues which are the subject of moral concern, from poverty, hunger and disease to pollution, organic farming and other 'green' topics, and on debates about how such problems might be addressed. Geography is also engaged with those particular parts of the world in which new institutional arrangements are being formed, in Eastern Europe, South Africa and Israel/ Palestine, for example. In short, students of geography should be particularly well informed about the background conditions against which people attempt to resolve conflict over what is right, or what should be a good way to live. (p. 274)

Suggested Lesson Plan

Developing the Moral Sentiments and Moral Judgment While Thwarting Cultural Narcissism

1. Teacher uses simulation/role play. Students in groups are assigned to select one student to represent the group in one of the following roles: U.S. secretary of state, president of Russia, foreign minister of the Peoples Republic of China, and president of a newly established third world country. Students must decide what type of foreign aid to supply to this third world country, how it is to be distributed, and the motivation driving these initiatives (Craig, 1994).
2. Teacher-guided discussion of the moral sentiments. Wilson's four sentiments are introduced on an overhead transparency.
3. Journal entries: Students analyze how duty, fairness, self-control, and sympathy were part of their motivation for supplying and/or justifying their receiving foreign aid; students share journal responses the next day.
4. Teacher presents elements of cultural narcissism on an overhead transparency. In small groups, students examine how these narcissistic elements could compromise foreign aid efforts and distributions to this new country.
5. Students bring in clippings from newspapers and weekly news magazines focusing on selected geographical topics, for example, hunger, disease, pollution, homelessness, and poverty. In small groups, students discuss how the moral sentiments are reflected in their motivation to help these nations address these problems (Smith, 1995).

6. In small groups, students search the Internet for articles and information related to their selected topics. Here, Amnesty International's web site (see <http://www.amnesty.org/>) is informative and user-friendly; it lists countless examples of human rights violations, including those relating to famine, disease, and so on. Students examine how the moral sentiments might prompt efforts to alleviate the issues cited in the Amnesty International web site.

Applying the Full Moral System: Refining Self-Understanding and Social Cognition

1. Journal entries: Students reflect upon how hunger, disease, homelessness, poverty, and pollution occur in their own communities. Possible questions: How are these problems being addressed by local government and/or social agencies? Have you witnessed these problems first hand? How have your direct experiences with these events prompted a deeper understanding of yourself? Of others?

2. In small groups, students share journal entries and generate a list of social problems, which they then prioritize on an overhead transparency.

3. Large-group discussion: Each group presents transparencies to the class. The three most cited problems are identified. Students develop school-based strategies for community service that could directly alleviate these problems. Students examine how the forces of cultural narcissism could undermine their ability to persuade their peers to participate in these activities.

Analysis and Discussion: Blending Idea and Product Technologies

Just as idea technology blended with product technology in the previous activities in American social history, a similar blending occurs in the above instructional procedures, resulting in the reinforcement of geographical understanding as well as in the articulation of how the moral system functions to create prosocial behavior. This blending of technologies also assists students to understand how cultural narcissism can thwart refinements within the moral system and can sabotage prosocial conduct.

The use of role-play, an idea technology, illustrates the reinforcement of core concepts by referring to the enactive phase of Dale's Cone of Experience (Heinich et al., 1999). As students simulate these roles of national ministers debating human rights issues, they introduce emotional dimensions into the learning process, thereby generating a climate for more complete and long-term understanding (Sylwester, 1994). Role-play also enhances perspective-taking which can foster both self-understanding and social cognition. The various group activities offer additional perspective-taking opportunities, while providing contexts for sharpening student interpersonal intelligence. Likewise, such group learning gives students contexts for helping each other, thus improving concept mastery and moving students higher up within their respective zones of proximal development (Vygotsky, 1976). Bloom's cognitive domain, also an idea technology, guides numerous activities requiring application and analysis (Woolfolk, 1998).

While these idea technologies are cross-nourishing, they also interact with and cross-fertilize the product technologies within these activities. For instance, low-tech software (e.g. magazine clippings) can be highly motivational, with linkages to visual intelligence and to concept application. Similarly, the use of the Internet web site, an example of high-tech software, facilitates application and analysis as well as higher-level problem solving. Equally important, this product technology generates the baseline knowledge for further refinements within the moral system, particularly of the moral sentiments. And once more, as students apply elements of the moral system to graphics and web sites, they gain a greater understanding of these product technologies themselves, while simultaneously grasping how the moral system should operate in their own lives and in the broader society to support prosocial behavior and nurture moral conduct.

Historical Biography and Positive Narcissism

Social studies teachers frequently use historical biographies to place human faces on historical events, particularly on events from the distant past. Through such biographies, students are able to appreciate, for example, the personal physical challenges of the young Theodore Roosevelt and the male hegemony within the political arena faced by Elizabeth Cady Stanton. These depictions of human challenge and triumph, frequently accompanied by vivid personal narratives and detail, provide models of encouragement for adolescents who confront similar personal challenges as they negotiate their way through their teenage years. Historical biographies also provide baseline behavior against which adolescents can test their own strengths and limits in defining their self-understanding and in identifying future goals, occupations, and vocations.

Historical biographies are frequently assigned to emphasize the outstanding social and personal virtues of historical figures, although some teachers often use these same readings to highlight the protagonist's personal and social shortcomings. In either case, social studies teachers might also consider introducing the concept of positive narcissism within historical biography, a type of narcissism which, ironically, can be beneficial in nurturing prosocial behavior.

As explained in chapter 2, Goldberg (1980) argued that narcissism in its positive sense is the piston that drives human exploration and creativity. It is the force that inspires persons to cling tenaciously to beliefs and ideas that may run counter to the social order. Positive narcissism "is the unwillingness to be dissuaded, discouraged, and ridiculed against giving birth to the most audacious and grandiose projects" (Goldberg, 1980, p. 12).

With these perspectives in mind, teachers choosing to use Lasch's paradigm of cultural narcissism in teaching historical biography could also underscore how positive narcissism may have motivated such persons as Susan B. Anthony, Frederick Douglass, and Thomas Jefferson. Here, teachers need to emphasize that the passion of these persons for challenging the social order proceeded from their sense of duty to advance human equality and to confront the social injustices of those times that sabotaged justice and fairness. Such classroom discussion would clarify the concept of positive narcissism as well as illustrate how these moral feeling states can influence moral action and moral judgment. Ultimately, teachers should guide students in assessing the degree to which narcissistic impulses are positive, extending outward from the self in prosocial pursuits that can benefit the self and others.

Suggested Lesson Plan

Developing the Moral Sentiments and Moral Judgment

1. Students choose and read a historical biography (e.g., that of Theodore Roosevelt or Elizabeth Cady Stanton).
2. Using an overhead transparency, the teacher introduces the concept of the moral sense, citing Wilson's sympathy, fairness, duty, and self-control. In small groups, students brainstorm other possible inborn moral sentiments and rank these according to their value in contributing towards the development of a personality profile that would best serve the needs of a civilized society. Groups report rankings to the entire class using overhead transparencies. Acting as a scribe, the teacher summarizes results on the chalkboard as students report.
3. Teacher-guided discussion: Students identify overlaps within the sentiments and consolidate concepts. Open discussion of how these

sentiments can be used to formulate moral judgments. Teacher so-
licits topical examples of this process.

4. In groups, students examine the personality and actions of the
   historical figure that they read, noting examples of how moral
   sentiments may have prompted and influenced specific prosocial
   behavior.

5. Teachers intending to introduce the concept of positive narcissism
   should first present an overview of Lasch's thesis of cultural narcissism, displaying on an overhead transparency the characteristics of
   cultural narcissism. For homework, students bring in examples of
   cultural narcissism as reflected in magazine ads and TV commercials. These are shared in small groups the next day.

6. In small groups, students discuss how cultural narcissism has the
   potential of compromising the development and refinement of the
   moral sentiments.

7. Teacher presents on an overhead transparency Goldberg's (1980)
   concept of positive narcissism. Teacher-guided discussion of contemporary figures (e.g., from politics, athletics, media, etc.) who
   exhibit examples of positive narcissism and prosocial behavior in
   their conduct.

8. In small groups, students reexamine their historical biographies and
   look closely for examples of positive narcissism. Students can expand their knowledge of the selected historical figure by searching
   the Internet. "The Biographical Dictionary" (<http://www.s9.com/
   biography>) is a comprehensive source, providing biographies of
   more than 27,000 notable men and women who have shaped the
   ancient and modern world. Students would contrast the web site
   data to the previously read biography, citing overlaps and addi-
   tions, and they would also search for examples of narcissistic behavior within this web site data. Finally, students would compare/
   contrast the behaviors of their historical figure to the behavior of
   contemporary figures, again noting manifestations of negative and/
   or positive narcissism.

Applying the Full Moral System: Refining
Self-Understanding and Social Cognition

The Questioning-Circle System (Kindsvatter, Wilen, & Ishler, 1996) is an
especially effective strategy for refining critical thinking, for personalizing
understanding of concepts, and for nurturing the moral system, particularly self-understanding and social cognition. As presented in chapter 2,
the Questioning-Circle System guides students, first, to probe the subject

matter under discussion; second, to relate the matter to their own lives; and third, to connect the matter to an external reality separate from themselves. These three phases can also overlap, yielding, for example, a question that can blend the subject matter with both personal and external realities. Teachers using historical biographies can extend the previous historical biography activities by activating the Questioning-Circle System, a strategy that will simultaneously enhance both student self-understanding and social cognition.

1. Using an overhead transparency with diagrams, the teacher explains the Questioning-Circle System. See Figure 2. 1.
2. Student journal entries: Students apply the first three movements of the Questioning-Circle System to their reading of their historical biographies. For example: In the context of Elizabeth Cady Stanton's biography:
   a. The Matter: What were the three most significant reasons for Stanton's drafting the Declaration of Sentiments at the Seneca Falls Convention? (For text of document see <www.rochester.edu/SBA/declare.html>)
   b. Personal Reality: Have you personally experienced these three reasons (e.g., of gender prejudice) in your life? Cite examples. Have you personally experienced other forms of prejudice founded on power or social configurations similar to those identified by Stanton? Cite examples.
   c. External Reality: Have you witnessed others who were the objects of prejudice? Were the sources of this prejudice the same as or similar to those sources that motivated the prejudice towards you? Discuss.
3. In small groups, students compare journal entries and brainstorm ways to formulate questions that incorporate a blending of subject matter, personal, and external realities. For example, Are there ways of identifying sources of gender, racial, and religious prejudice which we have experienced that may be addressed through community projects? Such a question would be a blend of subject matter, personal, and external realities.
4. Teacher-guided discussion relating these blended questions to the moral sentiments and to moral judgment. For instance, which moral sentiments may have influenced student recommendations to organize community projects? Are these recommendations also moral? Explain.

Analysis and Discussion: Blending Idea and Product Technologies

As in the social history and the geography models, this paradigm for teaching historical biography illustrates once more how the blending of idea and product technologies reinforces learning as it fosters the moral system. There are various idea technologies present including Piaget's formal operations (1969); Bloom's cognitive domain (Woolfolk, 1998); Vygotsky's (1976) zone of proximal development; Gardner's (1983) multiple intelligence theory; Lasch's (1979) paradigm of cultural narcissism; Goldberg's (1980) paradigm of positive narcissism; and Damon's (1995) moral system.

As in the previously described lessons, the idea technologies here also complement each other (Bloom and Piaget; Gardner and Piaget) in unique blends that enhance understanding. However, the idea technologies above go beyond the functioning of such technologies in the previous two examples. For instance, the introduction of Goldberg's idea technology of positive narcissism adds a conceptual schema that challenges students to redirect their understanding of Lasch's thesis that cultural narcissism is necessarily negative. Here, the use of a low-tech product technology (magazine ads and TV commercials) and a high-tech product technology (an Internet web site) facilitates an understanding of the distinctions between positive and negative narcissism. Such distinctions are essential in having students appreciate how these two forms of narcissism can either compromise or encourage the development and practice of prosocial behavior and the moral growth that builds on this behavior.

Kindsvatter et al.'s (1996) Questioning-Circle System is also an idea technology that offers a context for developing both self-understanding and social cognition. Furthermore, the circle, as it is used in the described lesson plan, leads sequentially to the questions that can stimulate the moral sentiments and activate moral judgment. By engaging the entire moral system through the questioning circle, teachers can more easily illustrate how the instances of narcissism in the biography are positive or negative and how such manifestations can foster or thwart prosocial behavior. Finally, the blending of idea and product technologies here develops in the students' specific analytic habits of thought as well as confidence and interest in using low-tech and high-tech tools of learning.

Multiculturalism, Immigration, and Identity

Multicultural education, which is now included in some format in almost all public school curricula throughout the nation, provides immediate opportunities for raising issues that impact directly on the cultivation of prosocial behavior and on the formation of character best fitted for a participatory democracy. Multicultural education can also help students refine all components of the moral system. As Grant (1994) explained, "[M]ulticultural education is a philosophical concept and an educational process" (p. 4). Philosophically, it focuses on nurturing those ideals posited in many federal documents, such as the Declaration of Independence and the Constitution, that emphasize freedom, equality, and justice. As a process, multicultural education occurs in schools and "prepares all students to work actively towards structural equality in the organizations and institutions of the United States" (Grant, 1994, p. 4). Through classroom activities in history, culture, and literature, students learn how various racial, ethnic, religious, and gender groups influenced the culture, politics, and history of America. Such activities also "help students to develop positive self-concepts and to discover who they are, particularly in terms of multiple group membership" (Grant, 1994, p. 4).

While some multicultural programs have the potential of reinforcing group stereotyping (Ryan, 1993), most programs provide students a needed balance of self-understanding and social cognition: an understanding of themselves as individuals and as members of several groups, as well as an understanding of others as individuals and of others as members of groups to which the student does not belong. As explained in chapter 3, such understanding of the self and others is particularly critical during adolescence when a student's struggle with self-definition becomes amplified, and for some, even obsessive (Erikson, 1968). Additionally, such programs should ideally reveal the common thread of humanity that unites all peoples, a thread that is strengthened when all peoples are provided justice, freedom, equity, and equality. Because multiculturalism can expose breaches in these ethical and social principles, students' moral sentiments and moral judgment can be appealed to and refined as they devise strategies for addressing these violations of justice and affronts to human dignity.

In examining the numerous myths surrounding multicultural education, Grant (1994) noted that multiculturalism is not "a minority thing" (p. 5), and it should not be perceived as centering mainly on people of color. Nevertheless, because people of color and other disenfranchised groups have frequently been overlooked in school curricula, some social studies teachers unwittingly affirm this myth by allocating a disproportionate amount of instructional time exclusively to these peoples. While certainly such people within America and abroad have been denied their respective rights as citizens of the United States and of the world, other peoples throughout history have been treated similarly by the respective dominant cultures. Consequently, it may be helpful to examine issues of multiculturalism as part of a larger unit on immigration. In so doing, teachers can place multicultural issues in historical context, showing particularly that America was never really a *melting pot* of races and cultures. This approach would also reveal that the economic and social structures that today deprive so many disenfranchised people their rights were the same structures that in the nineteenth-century also deprived African Americans, Asian Americans, and many European Americans of their rights. By providing those students who are descendants of such peoples their lost history, teachers can refine the perspective-taking skills of all students, which, in turn, can lead to greater social cognition. Finally, such a historical overview that includes immigrant groups from throughout the world can again engage students in discussions that require the application of moral judgment, here again based on Wilson's (1993) moral sentiments of sympathy, fairness, duty, and self-control. From a cognitive perspective, such an approach would also show how, for example, different racial, ethnic, religious, and gender groups worked together in challenging structural prejudice. And such an approach would highlight the rich cultural contributions that all groups have made to the tapestry of American life.

Unit Template

What follows is an instructional template for teaching multiculturalism, immigration, and identity. It will span approximately ten days; however, curriculum constraints and availability of instructional resources, as well as student motivation, interest, and diversity within the class, will influence how this template will be applied. This unit could be taught within American history and could be infused within the frameworks of numerous texts, for example, Faragher, Buhle, and Czitrom's (1994) *Out of Many: A History of the American People* or Garrity's (1994) *The Story of America*. This unit could also be included in a geography/world cultures curriculum and be fitted to serve with various texts, for example, Schwarz and O'Connor's (1998) *Exploring a Changing World* or English's (1995) *Geography: People and Places in a Changing World*. Regardless of the text used, additional readings should be included to extend learning and to probe the core concepts that, in many texts, are embedded in historical-cultural snapshots of each immigrant group. One of the most effective collateral texts, which in some classes may serve as the primary reading of the unit, is Daniels's (1991) *Coming to America: A*

History of Immigration and Ethnicity in American Life. Published in paperback, the text is a comprehensive treatment of major immigrant groups and ethnic life in America. It includes photos and statistical graphs and tables, and it is easily within the readability level of most 11th and 12th graders. The instructional template below will refer to this text, although similar books such as Daniels's (1997) *Not Like Us: Immigrants & Minorities in Modern America, 1890–1924* and/or Sowell's (1981) *Ethnic America: A History* could also be used. Two excellent collateral sourcebooks for teachers are *A Different Mirror: History of Multicultural America* (Takaki, 1993) and *Speaking of Diversity: Language and Diversity in Twentieth-Century America* (Gleason, 1992).

Day One:
Entry: Set induction. Teacher-guided discussion of "ethnicity" and "nationality." The teacher prompts students to think about the concepts of ethnicity and nationality. As the teacher leads the interactive discussion, several students act as scribes, placing on the chalkboard clusters of responses about particular cultural and racial groups which may be expanded to include religious and gender groups. Sample questions may include: What is your ethnic and/or racial background? Can you remember when you first became aware of this background? Does your family observe any holidays, practices, or rituals related to your ethnic and/or racial background? Do other ethnic groups or Americans in general have stereotypical images of those of your ethnic and/or racial background? Teacher encourages students to explain their responses.

Closure: Teacher comments on how people are individuals who are influenced by various subcultures.

For homework: Journal entries. Students explore what it means to be an American. Possible questions could be: What are the characteristics of American culture? How can a person be both an American and a member of another ethnic group? Am I an American? Explain. Would I also describe myself with a "hyphen"? (e.g., African-American? Italian-American? German-American, etc.).

These activities generate a context for studying ethnicity and immigration, a context which later in the unit will provide the prior knowledge essential for probing more sophisticated concepts. Moreover, these activities are driven by numerous idea technologies: Piaget's formal operational thought; Bloom's application, analysis, and evaluation; and Gardner's intrapersonal intelligence. The activities also address Erikson's adolescent conflicts in identity which have immediate implication for refinements within both self-understanding and social cognition.

Day Two:
In small groups, students share and discuss journal entries. Each group generates and presents a graphic web of their discussion results either using an overhead transparency or a software program such as *Inspiration* (1988–99) which would help them organize their concept mapping.

Closure: Teacher-guided discussion synthesizing and clarifying core concepts from the presentations.

The sharing of journal entries activates perspective-taking, while the formation of webs reinforces spatial skills (Gardner, 1993). As a synthesizer of the concept webs, the teacher can draw attention to the reciprocity between self-understanding and social cognition (Baldwin, 1902).

Days Three, Four, Five, Six, Seven:
Ethnic research: Students choose an ethnic group to research. Ideally, this would *not* be their own ethnic and/or racial background. The diversity of the class would influence the teacher's decision regarding how this process would be structured. Students are clustered according to their research choice. Ideally, the student groups would vary in size between five and seven participants.

Research Project Activities:

1. Students read from relevant chapters from Daniels's (1991) *Coming to America* or from a similar text.
2. Each student group views a videotape on their selected ethnic/racial group. An effective source is the Schlessinger Video Productions' *The Multicultural Peoples of North America* video series (1993). Each tape is approximately 30 minutes and presents a specific ethnic/racial group. In general, each tape explains why the group came to America, the various challenges encountered, strategies used to overcome these challenges, contemporary examples of successful Americans from this group, and how these modern Americans keep their respective ethnic/racial traditions alive.
3. In small groups, the students examine how the video supplemented the readings. Were there overlaps of information and/or contradictions? Students also discuss what "counts" as historical data that undergird claims made about the ethnic/racial group. Is this data reliable? Is it believable?
4. Journal entries. Each student individually analyzes how structural and/or institutional prejudices kept the ethnic/racial group from achieving freedom, equality, equity, and justice. Later, in their groups,

students discuss if similar prejudices today deprive ethnic/racial groups of these rights and principles.

5. In their research project teams, students use the Internet to visit the Ellis Island web site [www.1-channel.com/features/ellis/]. This web site includes hot buttons to: Historical Overview, The Journey, Through America's Gate, Ellis Island Today, the Oral History project, and the Ellis Island Cookbook. The site also features icons that are linked to audio clips (WAV format) of the recollections of some of the people who were processed through Ellis Island. Students should also consult another web site (<http://www.cmp.ucr.edu/exhibitions/immigrant_id.html>), which presents numerous photos of Ellis Island as well as pictures of various immigrant groups arriving and being processed.

6. Project Closure: Groups present their ethnic/racial group to the class through a combination of strategies: overhead transparencies, with accompanying outlines and Q&A; role-play and videotaping of an Ellis Island processing procedure; and/or talk-show format, which also may be videotaped, featuring "interviews" with immigrants that focus on their impressions of America, on the challenges they confronted in America, and on the strategies used to cope with these challenges.

These activities, which span approximately five days, demonstrate the operation of almost all idea technologies presented thus far in this chapter, from Dale's Cone of Experience and Gardner's multiple intelligences to Bloom's cognitive taxonomy, Piaget's formal operational thought, and Vygotsky's zone of proximal development. They also utilize various low-tech and high-tech product technologies, including transparencies, printed texts, audio clips, web sites, and videos. These four days maximize the systemic interpenetration of these technologies, ideally resulting in higher levels of cognitive understanding that are buttressed by affective interaction with the core concepts. Such affective interaction heightens student enthusiasm, spurs interest, and increases both short-term and long-term concept understanding and retention (Sylwester, 1994).

Days Eight, Nine, and Ten

1. Teacher-guided presentation and interactive discussion of Wilson's moral sentiments.

2. In small groups, students brainstorm other potential sentiments that guide prosocial behavior. Results are generated on a graphic web

that each group presents to the class on a transparency. In-class student journal response: Each student analyzes how the sentiments may have prompted their ethnic/racial group to band together to help the group (e.g., the Chinese Consolidated Benevolent Association and the National Association for the Advancement of Colored People) and how other ethnic/racial groups and/or individuals from these groups assisted newly arrived ethnic/racial groups. Students share journal entries.

3. Teacher guides discussion, which is designed to synthesize journal results. Teacher presents Lasch's thesis of the culture of narcissism, using transparencies to outline central traits (described in chapter 2). Open discussion of how cultural narcissism can compromise the prosocial behavior based on Wilson's moral sentiments. Student journal: Students explore how the culture of narcissism, in affecting a person's behavior, may influence that person to deny the basic rights, freedoms, and dignity to someone from an immigrant or disenfranchised group. In small groups, students share journals. Teacher-guided discussion of results of journals focusing on how individuals and institutions can address the culture of narcissism, especially in terms of how it threatens the freedom and justice of all people.

These three days are critical to the refinement of the moral system. The activities in days 1 through 7 fostered self-understanding and social cognition in the context of ethnicity and social cognition. Days 8 through 10 build on these developments in guiding students to make moral judgments, judgments deriving largely, but not exclusively, from Wilson's moral sentiments and judgments that can be influenced by the forces of narcissism within the culture.

Extending the Unit:

Depending on time and resources, teachers may choose to include the following activities which feature examples of idea and product technology. These activities may be inserted appropriately in the above model to extend cognitive and prosocial learning.

1. Students interview relatives and/or friends about the preparation of ethnic foods. They then consult the Ellis Island web site and explore the "Ellis Island Cookbook," searching for similar ethnic recipes. Journal entry: Students compare and contrast the recipes from the two sources. Students could also use their newly acquired

knowledge of food groups indigenous to the "immigrant country of origin" to make their recipes for a unique dish to be shared in class.

2. Field trips to various ethnic sites such as an African American Museum, a Jewish American Museum, a Swedish American Museum or to an agency designed to help immigrants adjust to American culture. Journal entry: Students relate these learning activities to the closure activities in day 7 above.

3. Field trip to large metropolitan art museum which features paintings capturing the immigrant or minority experience. Journal entry: Students relate these artistic depictions and themes to the closure activities in day 7 above or may opt to create their own artwork to depict their own family's cultural heritage using a medium of their own choice, pastel, computer-generated, and so on.

4. Students use the Internet to make e-mail contacts with "electronic pen-pals" (See <www.Stolaf.edu/ntework/iecc/related-sources.html>). After finding a pen pal, students engage in a semester-long e-mail writing project that introduces them to this particular world culture as seen through the eyes of an "adolescent contemporary." Students develop portfolios that capture the essence of this culture by combining e-mail exchanges with previously studied material on ethnic groups.

Teachers choosing to extend the unit by using most or all of the above activities will be supported by numerous blendings of idea and product technologies. The first activity focuses on a web site that serves as a source for baseline cultural data (Piaget, Bloom) which students compare and contrast to additional data (Bloom). This activity also provides for a capstone production of a creative recipe (Bloom). The second activity engages students with first hand experience with ethnicity and immigration (Dale see Heinich et al., 1999). The third activity is structured around Dale's iconic phase of experience, and it is further supported with Gardner's spatial intelligence. The fourth activity uses e-mail to assist with student cultural "de-centering" (Piaget) and to foster, once more, greater social cognition and self-understanding (Damon). All of these activities extend learning by supplementing the core concepts of the unit and by nurturing various displays of prosocial behavior.

Conclusion

Nyberg and Egan (1981) in *The Erosion of Education: Socialization and the Schools* present a conceptual analysis of "education" and "socialization." Their analysis impacts directly upon how cultural narcissism, technology, character education, and social studies content interpenetrate each other. Commenting that education and socialization require "different criteria in justifying curriculum activities," Nyberg and Egan observed that socialization is "regulated by the criterion of direct relevance or utility to social praxis," whereas education proceeds from the criterion of "personal enrichment" (1981, p. 2). In short, "Being socialized . . . makes life in society possible; being educated makes it more worthwhile" (1981, p. 2).

Illustrating these distinctions, Nyberg and Egan (1981) remarked that teaching children to read can be justified because literacy is a social necessity, but learning to read with aesthetic acuity and to write with style are merely desirable. Similarly, teaching children history can be justified because of its socializing effects, particularly as such academic study guides students to understand how contemporary society functions and how it developed from earlier social configurations. Such knowledge, all part of the socializing criterion, intentionally guides students to be better citizens and, at least theoretically, to contribute thoughtfully to a participatory democracy. In contrast, a sophisticated historical consciousness cannot be justified on social utility, but it "may be justified on the grounds of educational value" (p. 2).

The activities contained in this chapter attest to Nyberg and Egan's claim that "almost all activities in schools have socializing and educational dimensions" (1981, p. 3). In one sense, these activities can enrich a student's personal life because they are designed to reveal deeper insights into the self and into others. These moments of "personal enrichment" are directly prompted by the blending of various idea and product technologies. Additionally, the blending of technologies can foster a more refined historical consciousness, especially as students respond to the vivid pictorials of colonial life, photos of Ellis Island and the immigrant experience, and related Internet web sites.

While having the potential of enhancing a student's historical consciousness, as well as contributing to her content mastery, these activities have socializing effects. But rather than having some "utility to social praxis" which may lead students to replicate social norms, these activities are more socially reconstructive. They have been designed to prompt greater prosocial awareness in those academic and interpersonal contexts where cultural narcissism has diluted such awareness. As such, these activities would help to nurture all components of the moral system and, one would hope, result in more consistent patterns of moral conduct.

Chapter Seven

Character Education in the Mathematics and the Science Classroom

Character education seems to be a natural complement to the teaching and learning of English and social studies but may appear to be less of one when it is related to the more technically oriented disciplines of mathematics and science. Nevertheless, what math or science teacher, if given the opportunity, would not want to foster student prosocial behavior and impede cultural narcissism? Consequently, this chapter suggests ways in which math and science teachers can capitalize upon those periodic, teachable moments that arise naturally from the subject matter being taught, student curiosity, the popular media, community concerns, and so on, in order to promote character education while simultaneously remaining true to the intellectual pursuits of their disciplines as well as the developmental needs of their adolescent learners (Posamentier & Stepelman, 1999).

This chapter is divided into two parts: the first is a lesson plan involving mathematics (analytic geometry) that can be taught in a typical algebra I or II secondary classroom; while the second part addresses the scientific curricula of high school biology, more specifically ecosystems.

Mathematics and Character Education

The initial component of this section addresses the National Council of Teachers of Mathematics' (NCTM) assertion that

> a variety of instructional methods should be used in classrooms in order to cultivate students' abilities to investigate, to make sense of, and to construct meanings from new situations; to make and provide arguments for conjectures; and to use a flexible set of strategies to solve problems from both within and *outside mathematics* [italic added]. (pp. 127–128)

Secondary math educators may find that Damon's (1995) moral system, self-understanding, social cognition, moral sentiments and moral judgment, provides one such powerful *extra-mathematics* strategy to use in addressing real-world applications emphasized in many contemporary math classrooms. Such applications provide pragmatic contexts which, in turn, foster content-specific teaching and learning opportunities that encourage students to question their own values, their community's needs and goals, and the mathematical content itself.

Bitter and Pierson (1999), in *Using Technology in the Classroom*, suggest that "[t]he development of students as thinkers, problem-solvers and creators require[s] teachers to create and invent scenarios and projects in which students work with ideas, symbols, and abstractions" (p. 4). Therefore, it is in this spirit that the following lesson plan is proffered. Intended to complement the secondary math educator's repertoire of real-world applications (NCTM, 1989, Standard 1, p. 137), this plan, entitled *A Calculated Decision,* may be implemented toward the end of a first-year algebra class, or in a second-year algebra class where students have some familiarity with plotting *x*- and *y*- variables. The lesson is suited for classes where students are learning to use table functions on a graphing calculator. The plan may extend from three to four days depending upon student ability, curriculum flexibility, and so on. It is intended to take place over three 50-minute periods; however, it could be easily adapted for intensive or block schedules. Specifically, this sample scenario is designed to develop not only a greater familiarity with two-dimensional graphing and table functions, but also a comprehension of and appreciation for Wilson's (1993) moral sentiments by conjoining problem-based learning with ethical decision making. Moreover, the plan incorporates educational technology (see chapter 4 for further discussion of idea and product technologies) in order for students to "explore, formulate, and test conjectures, prove generalizations, discuss and apply the results of their [mathematical] investigations (NCTM, 1989, p. 128). In addition, this lesson addresses the following *National Educational Technology Standards* (2000): Mathematics Standards which incorporate the "Discussion Draft" (p. 292) of the NCTM's 1998 Principles and Standards for School Mathematics:

• Standard 2: Patterns, Functions, and Algebra
• Standard 5: Data Analysis, Statistics, and Probability
• Standard 6: Problem Solving

- Standard 8: Communication
- Standard 9: Connections
- Standard 10: Representation

Lesson Plan: A Calculated Decision

Part 1

Drawing upon Gardner's (1991, 1999) notion of entry points, begin the lesson using a personal story, a narrational entry, that highlights pet ownership, pet injury or illness, and the subsequent need for veterinary assistance. Teachers may want to share elements of their personal lives by bringing in photographs (Why not use digital photos that can be imported into Microsoft's *PowerPoint* (1995) electronic presentation program?) of their own pets or the following scenario may be recounted.

Forty years ago Freckles, a beloved brown spotted spaniel, became critically ill and had to be "put to sleep." During the 1960s, medical options were limited; thus, Freckles was euthanized. If Freckles were alive today, however, other medical options would be possible. Yet with such technological advances come difficult decisions involving financial and emotional considerations.

Using this brief narrative as a springboard for interactive discussion, the teacher raises the following questions that address higher cognitive levels of learning (Kindsvatter et al., 1996): How much is Freckles's life worth? Can the cost of the dog's medical treatment ever become prohibitive? The teacher then poses the following probes:

- Should the decision to get medical treatment for any animal be based solely upon financial considerations? What other factors should be considered?
- Are there mathematical tools that can help us make up our minds as to whether or not we should save the animal? Should such a decision be made solely based upon a mathematical cost-benefit analysis?
- While calculating the cost for medical treatment, how do moral and emotional variables interact with logical/mathematical reasoning?

During the interactive discussion the teacher uses *PowerPoint* (1995) to introduce Wilson's (1993) four moral sentiments, fairness, empathy, duty, and self-control, in order to provide students with an ethical framework, an *idea technology*, for contemplating such dilemmas.

Part 2

At the conclusion of the narrational entry the teacher presents the following problem to the students:

> Your family has a tough decision to make quickly. An injured, but affectionate, stray puppy wanders into your back yard and you are concerned about its welfare. It looks as if an automobile hit it. So you consult with your local veterinarian, who examines the animal and determines that it has a serious medical condition which will result in the puppy's demise if it is not addressed expediently. The vet briefly outlines the following important choices:
>
> *Option One* involves minimal medical treatment, and incurs a $50 fee that is used to put the puppy to death immediately at the clinic in a humane fashion.
>
> *Option Two* involves extended treatment costing $150; the puppy will probably recover almost all of its normal functioning and live for five years in your home at your expense costing $15 per month. However, from the beginning of year three onward the dog will require medications at a total cost of $20 per month. At that point the dog will need three additional trips to the vet per year beyond the usual annual visit. The veterinary fee is estimated at $25 per visit. For example, students would need to calculate the following for themselves: Year one: $150 initial cost plus yearly maintenance cost (12 months @ $15 per month = $180 per year). This amounts to $330 total cost for year one. Year two: yearly maintenance of $180 plus one annual veterinary visit at $25 ($180 + $25). This amounts to a total cost of $205 for year two. Years three through five: annual maintenance @ $180, plus one yearly veterinary visit @ $25, plus $240 additional expenses for medication (12 months @ $20 per month), and an additional $75 veterinary fee (3 visits @ $25). This amounts to a yearly cost equaling $520 ($180 + $25 + $240 + $75 = $520).
>
> *Option Three* costs $400 for the initial treatment; the puppy will recover fully and, as long as it is given medication for one year costing an additional $20 per month, it will probably live another 15 years. The puppy will reside in your home at your expense. The cost of feeding the animal is estimated $15 per month. During the first year the dog will require four visits to the vet at $25 each in order to monitor its progress. Beginning with the second year these visits will be reduced to one annual visit. Similar to *Option Two*, students need to calculate specific costs per year.
>
> In addition to monetary considerations suggested in each of the four options you must also consider how the following ethical factors, namely, the four moral sentiments: sympathy, duty, fairness, and self-control, function in your family's decision making.

In order to solve this problem have the entire class input the annual cost and life expectancy variables into their graphing calculators to generate *baseline visual representations* for each of the three options delineated above. Teachers may also graph the data cumulatively, if they so choose. Teachers create several small teams of three to four students apiece. These teams will act as a family to resolve the presented dilemma.

Each team receives a snapshot description of their *family*. (Because of varying class sizes, there may well be two or more teams who share the same family description.)

Family Description A has accrued no debt and has a yearly gross income of $90,000. In this two-parent working family there are six children, two of whom will attend college within two years.

Family Description B is a family of five with a gross income level of $57,600 per year. Grandmother has a slight allergy to pet dander. The oldest child is extremely fond of animals and hopes to become a veterinarian.

Family Description C is a single parent family of three children. Mom was recently laid off from her job. Unemployment benefits of $485 per month will start in eight weeks.

Each student team, as a family, must determine a single monetary value to assign to the aggregate *moral sentiment variable*. For instructional purposes the teacher may want to identify an "acceptable" monetary range per year to put on that moral sentiment value, for example $0 to $1500. Agreement on such a single monetary value will, of necessity, require considerable discussion. Students will need to debate carefully how one goes about equating the moral sentiments as a monetary entity. Remind students to frame their discussions in light of their respective family snapshots. After agreement is reached, each team then recalculates their initial *baseline visual representations* by subtracting their designated *moral sentiment variable* as a monetary value from the total cost per year. For example, if one student team determines that their family's *moral sentiment variable* is $250 per year, then the team's adjusted or sacrificial cost for the puppy for year one would be −$200 ($50 − $250) for *Option One*, $80 ($330 − $250) for *Option Two*, and $670 ($920 − $250) for *Option Three* (See Figure 7.1).

Each student team is to decide collectively which option is "best," providing a logical/mathematical as well as a moral rationale for its decision. Moreover, students need to recognize that their graphs may dip below the x-axis (as illustrated in Figure 7.1), and whenever it does, it represents a particularly acute moral sacrifice. Whenever the bar dips below the x-axis there is no financial sacrifice but there is a moral sacrifice. Whereas, when the bar remains above the x-axis, there is a financial sacrifice but no corresponding moral sacrifice for the family. Thus, students will confront the fact that whatever they choose to do at a practical level to sustain

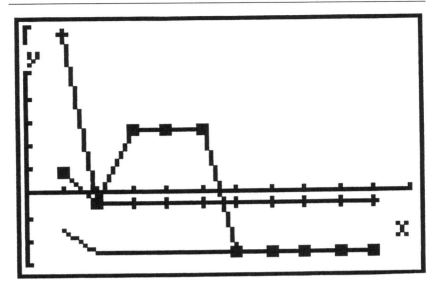

Figure 7.1 Illustration of options 1, 2, and 3 across 10 years where moral sentiments are valued at $250.00 for each year. Note where graph dips below the x-axis to demonstrate dissonance between family's stated value for moral sentiments and family's option choice.

financial viability may be strongly at odds with what they would choose to do from a moral stance. Here, the teacher may want to point out to the class that, even in mathematics, there is not always one "right" answer; rather, there may be several valid answers. Finally, teams gather as class, compare, and perhaps debate their respective solutions. The teacher may choose to project onto a large screen the students' graphs, using a LCD projection panel that connects directly to the graphing calculator itself.

The teams could reach various possible conclusions. For example, one team working with family description A (with $90,000 and five children) might decide to euthanize the puppy. They might explain that, even as a family that weighted the moral sentiments heavily (moral sentiments valued at $700 per year), the family's money was needed to support one of the precollege adolescents who required SAT tutorials. Another team working with family descriptor C (whose mother was recently unemployed) might weight the *moral sentiment variable* at $150 and decide that the family could support the puppy for three years, hoping that mom would be employed at that time when the veterinary expenses will change. This team may believe that money is less important than a sentient creature. They recognize that the initial level of expense would subside within a relatively short amount of time and that they would be able to enjoy the dog's companionship for a longer period of time. A team with family descriptor B (earning $57,600) might value the moral sentiments at $400 and choose *Option Three*. They may raise initial concerns about Grandmother's allergies, but because her allergies were mild the group felt that it was more important to save the puppy, thus providing the aspiring vet of the family with hands-on experience working with a needy animal.

Part 3

At this point the teacher may identify two teams who share the same family snapshot but who value the *moral sentiment variable* differently and choose different solutions to the dilemma. Teachers can share their students' collective graphic representations on a large screen using a LCD projection panel. Teachers can use this particular figure as an additional springboard for discussion and lesson closure. At this point, it may be helpful to reframe the initial probes used on day 1 of the lesson:

- Was your team's final decision regarding whether or not to get medical treatment for the puppy based solely upon financial considerations? What other factors did your family consider?
- How did the graphing calculator help your family clarify the cost and life expectancy variables? How did the mathematical information influence your final decision?
- How did the moral sentiments influence your final decision?

At the lesson's closure the teacher should point out how other real-life dilemmas, analogous to the one they have been working on for the past few classes, require similar types of reflective analyses. What may ostensibly appear to be a purely financial or emotional determination may not be so, when one recognizes all of the variables that are factored into a reasoned final decision. The teacher should further remark that in our world today many families face even more gut-wrenching, complex health care decisions, which affect not only individuals personally, but businesses, communities, and governments at the societal level as well. There are often no single easy answers.

Alternate Scenarios

In order to reinforce, challenge, and refine students' mathematical thinking and graphing capabilities, teachers may wish to modify this problem-solving scenario by altering variables. For instance, teachers may want to change some specific characteristics of the dog itself. It could, for example, be named Stevie, the trusted Seeing Eye dog who has lived with his 15-year-old owner for three years; or Charlie, the faithful family companion to a widowed dad and three children who recently suffered the loss of their mom from cancer. Dogs such as Stevie and Charlie serve vital social roles in their respective homes; therefore, such roles create an additional variable that the students must contend with. Students now must determine the value of the animal's role to the family. Similar to the moral sentiments, this variable can be assigned a monetary value.

Analysis and Discussion

The teacher's role during this lesson is multifaceted. The teacher provides a context within which to assess the accuracy of the students' mathematical work as well as to cultivate their four-component moral systems, namely, the tandems of moral judgment and moral sentiments, as well as self-understanding and social cognition (see chapter 3 for further discussion of the moral system and cultural narcissism).

By recounting Freckles's story and displaying photographs of the dog itself, the teacher provides a multimodal narrational entry into a mathematics lesson. By sharing personal stories coupled with visual photographs and the *PowerPoint* presentation the teacher will more likely address a wider range of student learning styles (Guild & Garger, 1998) and intelligences (Gardner, 1991; 1999), and appeal to those students who may not possess mathematical preferences or strengths, but who nonetheless are captivated by visual/spatial stimuli as well as interpersonal relationships. The probes used during the set induction provide a systematic structure (Kindsvatter et al., 1996) to introduce the moral sentiments as part of the decision-making process. Moreover, such probes help students recognize that many variables interact when tough decisions must be made.

The part of the problem-based instructional activity which asks the student teams to assign a monetary value to an abstract concept, *the aggregate moral sentiments variable*, requires that the learners explore their individual (and collective) values for the moral sentiments, establish a single monetary cost, and then present a rationale for the specific amount their respective teams have determined. Such an activity promotes self-understanding as well as social cognition. When the teams reach consensus regarding monetary values for fairness, duty, empathy, and self-control, they must negotiate with one another, acknowledging each other's viewpoints. Grappling with such difficult concepts necessitates that students possess a thorough understanding of each moral sentiment in order to make well-informed moral judgments. Reaching such a consensus is accomplished through compromise and negotiation, two processes that help promote prosocial behavior and thwart cultural narcissism.

Later in the lesson, when students are faced with deciding the fictitious puppy's future, they must balance their objective financial calculations and family budgetary limitations, then adjust that decision, taking into account the moral sentiments value. When a student team places a high monetary value on the *moral sentiments variable* yet, due to family income and/or special familial needs, chooses not to offer treatment for the puppy, learners experience cognitive and moral dissonance. Presented with such confounding variables, students may decide to renegotiate the agreed upon single moral sentiments value and/or engineer alternative solutions so that they more comfortably resolve the ethical dilemma. At that point the teacher continues to serve as mentor for both the logical/ mathematical as well as moral recalculations, helping students to recognize how the mathematical information, illustrated by the electronically generated graphs, illuminates the rational and emotional decision-making components.

The lesson offers students opportunities to appreciate peer viewpoints—namely, their other "family" members. When exploring a moral dilemma together, students engage in a meaningful learning activity, a context that fosters not only personal awareness (self-understanding), but also perspective-taking (social cognition). The interplay between these two facets of the moral system may, in turn, facilitate prosocial behavior. In addition, when students extend their investigations more deeply in order to examine how other teams respond, teams who share the same family backgrounds but value the moral sentiments differently and choose other options for the puppy's outcome, students need to reconcile how, given the same mathematical data and background situations, those teams can hold widely different perspectives and determine different solutions. In exploring the differences and similarities among such team decisions, students may need to reconcile these new perspectives with their own.

It should be added that initially the *moral sentiment variable* as a concept and as it used in these activities may appear reductionistic, mechanical, and even passionless. But this is not the case. And to infer that the *moral sentiment variable* is solely cognitive is only half the picture. As a mathematical variable, it is designed to reinforce higher-order quantitative thinking, but equally important, the *moral sentiment variable* is affective, designed to actually stir students' moral feeling states. In fact, the hypothetical scenarios requiring applications of this variable infuse the moral sentiments directly into the ensuing moral deliberations. Participating in these activities, students would be thrust into those uncomfortable feeling states described by Kagan (1994) that would prompt action-leading students out of these uncomfortable states (see chapter 3 for Kagan's discussion of this process). It is then through the interpenetration of the moral sentiments, self-understanding, and social cognition that students would be guided to exercise their moral judgment, a process that would also draw them out of these uncomfortable feeling states (e.g., by requiring applications of sympathy and fairness) and thus into more emotionally comfortable, prosocial states.

In conclusion, throughout *A Calculated Decision* students explore Wilson's four moral sentiments and base their "real-life" decisions, at least in part, upon them. Furthermore, by blending Damon's moral system with mathematical problem solving and role-playing, teachers can help students realize how so-called rational decisions are neither necessarily absolute nor wholly cognitive, and how they, as learners, can understand how systematic moral systems inform as well as enrich the lives of human beings.

Science and Character Education

Similar to mathematics and other disciplines that are taught in U.S. high schools, national committees have created guidelines and standards to promote educational reform in order "to produce a nation that is more scientifically literate" as well as "to make science more relevant for students, giving them a useful science education" (Chiappetta, Koballa, and Collette, 1998, p. 23). For instance, the American Association for the Advancement of Science (AAAS), in its Project 2061 initiative, stated that there is a

> critical need to produce a scientifically literate society so that individuals can deal with the problems they will face in the new millennium. . . . However, it will take an educated society, versed in science and technology, to comprehend societal problems and to deal effectively with them. (Chiappetta et al., 1998, p. 28)

In order to promote science education, works such as Project 2061's *Benchmark for Science Literacy* (AAAS, 1993) listed not only K-12 student learning outcomes, but also iterated the need for teachers to employ varied instructional methods as well as multiple and varied assessment measures. Similarly, the *National Science Education Standards*, formulated by the National Research Council (NRC), stressed the need to reconcile fast-paced scientific advancements with mutable societal needs, calling attention to what the NRC refers to as *Changing Emphases*. Specifically, the council recommends that science teachers put "less emphasis on studying subject matter disciplines for their own sake" and put "more emphasis on learning subject matter disciplines in the context of inquiry, technology, science in personal and social perspectives, and history and nature of science" (National Research Council, 2000, online). In light of these complex interrelationships between science and technology, and education and society, one may propose that the secondary science classroom provides an especially appropriate "laboratory" in which teachers may nurture student character by blending idea technologies such as Damon's (1995) moral system with the study of biology. (See chapter 3 for an extended discussion of his moral system, and chapter 4 for a more detailed explanation of idea technologies as they relate to classroom instruction.)

Science teachers should conjoin subject matter content with contemporary societal mores, particularly when ethical issues arise naturally as a consequence of students' exposure to television broadcasts, reputable newspapers, the World Wide Web, or other popular media sources. As Cairney et al. (1998) pointed out:

> Students in biology who will spend most of their lives in the twenty-first century have a right to be exposed to societal issues that grow naturally out of science because it is within the societal context—not the scientific—that the average student will grapple with these problems. (p. T 27)

Oftentimes, societal issues revolve around bioethical dilemmas where provocative questions are raised regarding the appropriate use of emerging medical technologies. (Have students view, for example, the videotape of "On the Frontier", a *CBS News Sunday Morning* segment which was aired on February 6, 2000, or visit the CBS News web site entitled, "Testimony On Gene Therapy Deaths," available at <http://cbsnews.cbs.com/now/story/0,1597,156168-412,00.shtml>). Nelson (2000) rationalizes that bioethics should be taught to high school students for the following reasons:

> First, it helps them see the relevance of biology in their lives. Bioethics can make topics, such as fetal tissue transplantation, which feel "far away" to many adolescents immediate and compelling. . . . Through exploring situations like this, students realize that biology and its associated technologies touch everyone, not just people in the medical profession. Furthermore, the implications of these

ethical questions for the development of public policy and legislation help students understand that in order to be a responsible citizen in a democracy, one must be well informed about both scientific fact and theory, as well as a thoughtful decision maker. (<http://accessexcellence.org/21ˢᵗ/TL/TBE/>)

One way to help students become *thoughtful decision makers* is to provide them with a framework, such as Damon's moral system (1995), to guide their thinking. Therefore, the remainder of this chapter suggests ways in which teachers can introduce character education into any high school biology or life sciences curricular unit. To be used as a template, the following unit overview represents one way that character education can be addressed in the biology classroom.

Science Unit Overview

This four- to five-week life sciences unit on genetics and heredity addresses, among other things, the following concepts: genes and their chemical makeup, genetic codes for protein production, DNA and its relation to chromosomes and genes, genetic variations, and genetic engineering. Within the first week of the unit teachers can directly introduce and reinforce Damon's four-component moral system (1995). In subsequent classes, teachers should anticipate "teachable moments," instances when specific subject matter content they are responsible for "covering," such as genetic engineering, can be directly related to components of Damon's moral system. If the "teachable moment" does not arise, then teachers can promote class discussion by generating appropriate "preview" questions and highlighting relevant terminology before having their students watch the video, *The Human Genome Project* (Stonebarger, 1999), which not only describes how scientists unravel the genetic codes of human beings, but also explains the potential benefits and drawbacks of genetic screening and reconstruction. As the students watch the program, teachers can conduct "inter-viewing" mini-discussions, pausing the tape periodically to answer student queries or to clarify terms and concepts that may be pertinent or challenging, especially those dealing directly with bioethical considerations that scientists often grapple with. During the next few weeks, teachers should continue to look for opportunities to promote similar discussions involving bioethical concerns. (For more detailed explanation of how similar types of lessons may be taught, see chapter 5 and chapter 7). The remainder of this discussion, however, will focus upon the unit's proposed technology-infused assessment projects that require students to think critically about how the life sciences and moral decision making interact.

Technology-Infused Assessment Projects. Reflecting the progressive emphasis suggested by the *National Science Education Standards* (NRC, on-line), the following science projects are intended not to supplant traditional assessment instruments such as quizzes, labs, or unit tests; rather, they are meant to extend students opportunities to demonstrate their mastery of course content. As the assessment projects are introduced, teachers can devote additional class time in order to answer student questions regarding both the biology content and the moral system as they relate to the projects themselves. Providing project rubrics at this time should be especially helpful in clarifying any unresolved issues or questions. When teachers create assessment rubrics to accompany individual and collaborative projects, they should ensure that each rubric contains a self- or group-processing component (Johnson, Johnson, Holubec, & Roy, 1990, quoted in Kindsvatter, Wilen, & Ishler, 1996, p. 308). In addition, teachers should require all students, individually and/or collectively, to reflect upon how their work relates to bioethical decision-making, pointing out, when appropriate, how elements of Damon's moral system, such as the four moral sentiments, are addressed (see Figure 7.2). Further, teachers may refer to Kasman Valenza's article "Students and Teachers Alike Can Benefit from Rubrics" (2000) as well as Marzano, Pickering, and McTighe's *Assessing Student Outcomes* (1993) for additional rubric suggestions.

To help students become better citizens, master the material the have been studying, prepare for their unit test on heredity, and have a little fun as well, teachers may want to consider assigning a few or all of the following options. The first, *Peas in a Pod*, is developed more fully and thus can be used as a template. The remaining six options serve as points of departure so science teachers can elaborate upon their own problem-solving scenarios and accompanying rubrics, and tailor them to the specific needs of their learners as well as their designated curricula.

1. *Peas in a Pod.* Create a minimum three-page screenplay, a "dramedy" in which you and your classmates personify mature, garden variety pea plants that argue about whether or not they want to reproduce offspring (i.e., baby peas) who may or may not possess the specific traits they were hoping for, wrinkled or round. The text of the play must incorporate the following scientific terminology: genes, chromosomes, DNA nucleotides, recessive traits, meiosis, fertilization, dominant traits, probability, prediction, round seeds, wrinkled seeds, genotype, phenotype, homozygous,

Genetics and Heredity Projects: Sample Assessment Rubric

Group Members: Student 1: _____
                   Student 2: _____
                   Student 3: _____
                   Student 4: _____
                   Student 5: _____

4 = Superior Work: a model for other students in class to emulate
3 = Very Good: fulfilled all requirements in a competent manner
2 = Satisfactory: fulfilled most requirements, but problems or omissions remain
1 = Unsatisfactory: did not meet the minimum requirements

_____. *Scientific Literacy*: Evidence of content mastery related to your specific project as demonstrated in your final project and/or presentations. This includes issues such as accuracy of information, overall organization, use of supporting details, adequate development, and the quality of your written, graphic, and/or oral work.

_____. *Bioethical Reasoning*: Evidence that you justified, individually or collectively, your decision using one or more elements of Damon's moral system.

_____. *Collective and Individual Effort*: Evidence of collaborative support, individual accountability, effort, enthusiasm, and ability to meet deadlines, keeping lines of communication open throughout the project.

_____. *Reflection*: Evidence of a neatly typed one-page reflective journal entry that describes not only what you have learned as a result of your work, but also the strengths and weaknesses of your project or presentation. (Consider, for example, what you might do differently if you had another chance to do it again.)

Overall Score: _____

Figure 7.2 Genetics and Heredity Projects: Sample Assessment Rubric

heterozygous, hybrids, gametes, alleles, the principle of segregation, and Gregor Mendel. You may perform the play live in front of your classmates, or you may videotape, audiotape, and/or storyboard it, using your artistic talents along with technological tools such as digital cameras and computer printers. Be sure to use your project assessment rubric as a guide because it will not only keep you on track, but also inform you as to how you will be graded for your work.

2. *Invisible Danger.* You are desperately seeking a high-paying job, but are worried about not being hired because of an illness you have inherited. You show no visible symptoms of your disease; nevertheless, you are concerned: Will future employers hire you if they know about your condition or have access to your medical records?

   The dilemma: Do you disclose or conceal your condition? Using a point/counterpoint format, compose a series of journal entries in which you attempt to resolve your dilemma drawing upon both biological and ethical resources.

3. *Death Row Decision.* Ripped from today's newspaper headlines: *18-Year-Old to Receive Death Penalty!* Upon reading this news article it becomes clear that the only evidence found linking the accused to the actual crime was the defendant's DNA. As a law student, you are asked to imagine that you are going to defend this young person in court in front of a jury of his or her peers. Prepare the defendant's opening statement. Remember, you need to address the central ethical dilemma: Is it right to put someone to death when the only evidence the prosecution has is that which is linked to the defendant's DNA?

4. *Hello Stephen!* Stephen Hawking, renowned author and scientist, has a degenerative disease that leaves him wheelchair bound and dependent upon a computer-based voice synthesizer in order to speak. The dilemma: Should such a brilliant scientist as Stephen Hawking be cloned? Should any human being be cloned? What criteria should be used to decide such questions? Make your case.

5. *Mr. and Mrs. Eugene Altered.* Given the scientific advances that have been made in gene therapy, parents may soon be able to modify a child's genes in order to prevent future medical problems. The dilemma: Should genes, ones that may exacerbate addictions to drugs, alcohol, sex, or food, be altered? Make your case.

6. *TimeShifting.* Become a renowned life scientist of your choice. Suppose, for example, you chose to become Gregor Mendel. If you were to time travel to the twenty-first century, would you still be an advocate for the genetic alteration of crops or livestock? Would latter-day scientists advocate any or all contemporary extensions of their original research?

7. *Final Exam.* As you know, genetic testing, still in its infancy, continues to evolve; thus, scientific test results do not always yield cer-
tainty. In light of this, consider the following problem: Your mother
and her three sisters all suffered from breast cancer several years
ago; each required extensive chemotherapy and/or surgery but are
now "cancer survivors." Recently, your 24-year-old sister tested
positive for having a cancer-related gene; however, no other outward signs of cancer were detected during her exam. In your informed view, should your "cancer-free" sister have a double mas-
tectomy conducted as a preventative measure? Do the research,
then make your case.

Analysis and Discussion

Although educational technology permeates the entire life sciences unit
outlined above, it is in the assessment projects themselves that the blending of idea and product technologies becomes most potent. Each of the
projects contains the seeds of varied idea technologies such as Bloom's
taxonomy of educational cognitive objectives, Gardner's multiple intelligence theory, Johnson and Johnson's cooperative learning, Dodge's
WebQuest, and most notably Damon's moral system. Using these baseline
idea technologies, science teachers are encouraged to explore, adopt, and
creatively blend additional idea and product technologies other than those
mentioned here, ones with which they feel comfortable, ones that they
find to be classroom-tested, well researched, and effective.

By incorporating direct instruction, planned discussions, and problem-solving projects into the unit, as well as capitalizing upon the very
nature of the issues related to the topic, this genetics and heredity unit
provides high school biology students the opportunity to examine their
own ethical decision-making processes. Similar to the presentation of the
moral system in the mathematics section described earlier in this chapter,
the *PowerPoint* presentation that is used to introduce Damon's moral
system also may engage more learners by appealing to a range of learning
styles (Guild & Garger, 1998) and intelligences (Gardner, 1991, 1999).
Moreover, the learner's moral systems are actively engaged in solving
realistic problem-based projects. In agreement, Chiappetta et al. (1998)
acknowledge that "[s]cience teachers can address the moral reasoning of
their students by involving them in moral dilemmas in which students are
asked to reason through situations that may have personal relevance"
(p. 170). What is more, these projects enable teachers to use them as
entry point perspectives which "[place] students directly at the center of

a disciplinary topic, arousing their interests and securing cognitive commitment for further exploration" (Gardner, 1999, p. 172). More specifically, they serve as *social entry points* where students "can assume different roles, observe others' perspectives, interact regularly, and complement one another" (Gardner, 1999, p. 172).

Intended not only to assist learners in grappling with the complexities involved in any bioethical dilemma, each project is also critical in helping students become more aware of how their self-knowledge, social mores (social cognition), and moral sentiments influence how they form moral judgments (Damon, 1995) in resolving such problems. Interestingly, the moral sentiments alone can offer a powerful framework for students to use as they attempt to reconcile personal beliefs with scientific data, and personal beliefs with their peer groups as they attempt to reconcile bioethical dilemmas. For example, in the project entitled *Final Exam*, student groups need to reach consensus about how a sibling would support an older sister who is faced with a vital medical choice. But before group consensus is formed, students need to identify their own perspectives so that they can "view" the role-playing situation through a variety of lenses, lenses such as their sister's, the medical team's, and the family's. Such perspective-taking is essential so that students can negotiate with other group members. At the very least, learners must reconcile their own sense of empathy and concern for their sister with sufficient use of self-control so as to harness their own possible fears that they, too, may suffer a similar fate. Collectively, the four moral sentiments provide a concrete reference point whereby the individual students at first, and later the group, can wrestle with issues related to the cultural narcissism of "me-ness" versus the prosocial "we-ness" that is so important in a family's or a larger community's decision-making processes. After individual students have worked through their own solutions, they can then begin to question, compromise, and reach a consensual agreement with fellow group members. As with the *moral sentiment variable* used in the previously cited mathematics activities, the moral sentiments as used in the science classroom are intermingled with cognitive perspective-taking. However, once more, these science simulations and role-play activities are designed to stir the sentiments so that the ensuing feeling states can augment rational analysis within the moral decision-making process.

In *Final Exam*, as well as *Peas in a Pod* and *Mr. And Mrs. Eugene Altered*, science teachers can consider the value of using cooperative groups as a context for clarifying one's own views (self-understanding) and for recognizing others' points of view (social cognition). Within the

moral system, Wilson's four moral sentiments provide students with a
common ground upon which to examine their understanding of the biological subject matter content as they analyze ethical dilemmas embedded
in most of the other problem-based scenarios.

Although each of the projects places a specific emphasis on using
Damon's moral system as an idea technology, other idea technologies
provide additional filters so that students can first research and then examine critical content issues. For example, in *Death Row Decision* and
Invisible Danger teachers may embed Internet-based WebQuests "that
spark the imagination, solve problems, and promote discussion about
important issues" (Brown Yoder, 1999, p. 53). As an alternative to
WebQuests, students may conduct analogous "VideoQuests" using *The
Human Genome Project* (Stonebarger, 1999). Similar VideoQuests may
be constructed for *Hello Stephen!* using *Cloning: How and Why* (1998),
a video also distributed by Hawkhill Associates, Inc. Adapting Brown
Yoder's guidelines for composing WebQuests, teachers need to gather
relevant materials from a variety of sources including "texts, reference
books, videotapes, places, and people who may be useful or even essential resources" (p. 9).

Finally, each of the problem-based assessment projects requires students to function cognitively at a variety of "levels of learning" (Bloom,
Engelhart, Frost, Hill, & Krathwohl, 1956). For instance, in *TimeShifting*,
students not only have to investigate the accomplishments of renowned
life scientists (the comprehension and analysis levels), but also make inferences and draw conclusions (the evaluation and synthesis levels) regarding whether or not those same biologists would agree with current applications of their theories.

Conclusion

Although many secondary mathematics and science teachers may not
necessarily perceive character education issues as part of their day-to-day
classroom responsibilities, they certainly recognize the many problems
facing adolescents during this crucial period of their development. While
some of these problems can be addressed directly using so-called "objective" data gleaned from math and science textbooks, most educators fully
apprehend that many difficulties in contemporary society are complex
and multifaceted. Possible resolutions may require not only facts and figures but also careful moral or ethical analyses. Occasionally, academic
subject matter content and moral issues clearly intersect; this chapter

encourages teachers to capitalize on those points of intersection. Delineated throughout, the chapter suggestions represent points of departure for those mathematics and science teachers who recognize that their respective disciplines can serve as wellsprings for students to tap so that they can not only become more cognizant of their moral decision making, but also develop into better, more prosocial human beings.

PART III

AFTERWORD

The Cultural Narcissism, Technology, and Character Education Paradigm: Will It Work?

It is a truism in many quarters of corporate America that sales people are the best compensated because they ultimately are responsible for the financial well-being and for the growth of the corporation. They bring in the money. Corporate marketers are also essential because they package the product. They entice the public to buy. At bottom, however, while sales success can be measured in dollars, marketing success is more ephemeral. There may be some correlation between a TV commercial for green milkshakes in early March, but it is difficult to ascertain whether these ads necessarily caused increases in purchases of milkshakes on Saint Patrick's Day. The intent of the advertising campaign would suggest a correlation, but there may be other variables at work such as the cost of shakes and the ethnic composition of the community.

The same is true with character education programs. Most school administrators are comfortable with initiating academic programs, such as new approaches to teaching reading or mathematics, which may be measured quantitatively. Student performance data would verify whether the financial investment for materials and the teacher workshops to prepare for these programs were justified and defensible. On the other hand, while most administrators would probably concede that schools by their nature influence the shaping of a child's character, these same administrators might hesitate to support such formal programs within the curriculum. Moreover, school officials, and particularly those responsible for urban schools, might be dissuaded from initiating character education programs because of the marked diversity of values within the school community. Noting these issues, Rest pointed out that when a public school district even hints that it is doing research on character education, "that is likely to cause civil war in the district" (Lockwood, 1997, p. 35).

School administrators and school board members frequently give only qualified support for these programs because there is no substantive data base attesting to the overwhelming effectiveness of any one program. As Leming remarked: "When one is fighting for space in the curriculum, evidence is needed that goes beyond anecdotes, which is frequently what is provided by character educators. Instead, there is a pressing need for evidence that is objective and credible" (quoted in Lockwood, 1997, p. 30). Despite this lack of empirical data, Leming contended that those programs with the greatest promise tend to blend developmental insights into how children learn with current research on how children are socialized. He also stated:

> It is logical that effective programs should include the use of clear, developmentally appropriate language and meaningful examples of moral behavior. They should take note of demands by teachers, parents, and communities that children behave in appropriate ways. . . . Finally, effective character education programs need to include interesting, engaging activities for kids that focus on the desired behavior. (quoted in Lockwood, 1997, p. 25)

Leming's observations tend to confirm what other researchers have found: that while empirical data does not support the relative effectiveness of any one program, there appears to be evidence that certain techniques within specific programs are more effective than others in leading to desired prosocial outcomes, or at least in providing contexts out of which desired prosocial outcomes have the greater probability of appearing.

One of the most convincing longitudinal studies that assessed the effects of specific character-building techniques on children's prosocial behavior was the Child Development Project in California. This project examined the effects of a program that intermingled the behavioral, cognitive, and affective dimensions of character development. Specifically, the project combined "cooperative learning, teaching empathy through literature, positive role models, developmental discipline, involving students in helping relationships, and parental involvement" (Lickona, 1995, p. 159). By the conclusion of elementary school, students exposed to these strategies, in contrast to those who were not, exhibited the following:

1. Showed more spontaneous acts of helping and encouraging their classmates (a measure of the behavioral side of character);

2. Were better at thinking of prosocial solutions to hypothetical social conflicts (a measure of the cognitive side of character); and
3. Were more committed to democratic values such as the belief that all members of a group have a right to participate in decisions affecting the group (a measure of the affective or attitudinal side of character) (Lickona, 1995, pp. 159–160).

McDaniel's (1998) more recent evaluation of the effectiveness of various character education techniques echoed several of the strategies used in the Child Development Project, including cooperative learning, parental and community support, and peer involvement. In particular, cooperative learning has been shown to increase prosocial behavior and to enhance children's ability to take another's point of view (Kohn, 1990). Furthermore, unless ethics are grounded "within the particular community and cultural context of the learner, ethics remain abstract, outside the scope and experience of the learner, and ultimately irrelevant" (Matthews & Riley, 1995, p. 17). Finally, "schools that seem to have an impact on student character respect students, encourage student participation in the life of the school, expect students to behave responsibly, and give them the opportunity to do so" (Leming, 1993, p. 67).

McDaniel concluded her summary of effective strategies by emphasizing the merits of Antes and Norton's (1994) techniques, which she correlated to those methods that, according to research, have worked in schools. Among Antes and Norton's recommendations were:

- Relate educational experiences to students' lives providing opportunities for students to share their points of view;
- Develop cooperative activities in the community with service projects to help students develop a sense of responsibility and connection to the community as a whole;
- Encourage discussions with and among students concerning aspects of school life and how to interact with other people in the appropriate manner;
- Encourage students to think in complex ways about moral issues in life as they appear in the curriculum;
- Use reading and writing activities to encourage moral and ethical thought;
- Structure the learning environment so that it models democratic values and provides a safe environment for learning, sharing, and cooperating;

- Encourage self-discipline through cooperative interaction between persons in the learning environment;
- Use discussion, role-playing, and analytical and creative projects as a basis for critical thinking about values, attitudes, character traits, and moral issues;
- And, use cooperative learning activities to help students develop social and interaction skills (quoted in McDaniel, 1998, pp. 6–7).

This overview of effective character-forming strategies supports and relates directly to those activities contained throughout the Praxis chapters. In the larger context of the moral system, McDaniel's (1998) summary has produced a rich constellation of techniques that in concert would also refine students' self-understanding and social cognition, as well as their moral judgment and moral sentiments. It is therefore no surprise that these strategies have been identified in the research as effective ways of fostering character education since they are ultimately grounded in the components of Damon's (1995) moral system. McDaniel's (1998) summary is also significant because her own assessment of the purpose of character education relates directly to the moral system and especially to the interplay between social cognition and moral sentiments. She claimed that "the goal of character education should be to promote self-initiated behavior and for children to be reinforced by the good feelings of others" (p. 4). Eschewing extrinsic, physical rewards for prosocial behavior, McDaniel acknowledged the internal emotional gratification that comes with affecting the well-being of others. The emotional response that accompanies such perspective taking is grounded in one's own sense of sympathy and, depending on the context, perhaps even in one's sense of fairness and/or duty. In either case, McDaniel's comments verify once more how components of the moral system form the bedrock of moral conduct.

While questions of effectiveness may surround the character education debate, developmental and curricular issues also compromise the nurturance of character in many secondary classrooms. According to Leming, "about 80% of current programs do focus on elementary schools. . . . Perhaps 15% are junior high or middle school programs; less than 5% are in high school" (quoted in Lockwood, 1997, p. 27). Leming explained that the general culture of the lower grades tends to address socialization, personality development, and character development, whereas the culture of the upper grades tends to be "more impersonal, much more

mechanic . . . [and] . . . much more sterile, with the day's rigid sched-
ule punctuated by bells marking the end of class periods" (quoted in
Lockwood, 1997, p. 27). In high school, teachers typically "see 150 kids
a day in five classes of 30 kids" and are frequently "more concerned with
student scores on exams" (Lockwood, 1997, p. 27). In contrast, the relationships between teachers and children in lower grades tend to be more
intimate, where teachers gain daily insight into their children's personal
strengths and weaknesses and where the interactional dynamics often
approximate those of a family. This apparent neglect of character education in the upper grades is, in Leming's assessment, a paradox because
the prosocial attributes that were allegedly cultivated in the lower grades
must necessarily be refined later on as children enter the social and personal turmoil of adolescence. In short, if schools are truly serious about
producing prosocial, moral citizens, then classroom efforts must continue
throughout the entire K-12 curriculum.

The activities included in the Praxis section are designed to refine the
foundational prosocial behaviors established in the lower grades. Equally
important, these activities have been developed around a unified theme
that, in action, is focused and systematic. As such, the idea and product
technology paradigm that undergirds all of these activities represents a
marked advantage over the many other character education strategies
that have been described as a "hodgepodge" or a "grab bag" of activities
that often conflict with each other (Lockwood, 1997, p. 36). Instead, the
Praxis activities have been intentionally designed to refine each student's
moral system and to reveal the potentially caustic effects of cultural narcissism, while simultaneously enhancing student mastery of the academic
content prescribed by the curriculum. And while many of these activities
provide options for adjusting the content and pedagogy through extension and/or compression, these options are intended to address student
interests, abilities, and learning styles. Collectively, these options are clearly
not a grab bag of disconnected strategies.

Other Spheres of Adult Influence

The Praxis activities illustrated how classroom teachers can foster prosocial
conduct while raising student awareness of how negative features of cultural narcissism function in society and how these features may interfere
with the development of the moral system. Students may indeed find
these activities thought-provoking and enjoyable, and teachers too may

find the activities beneficial in pointing their students' prosocial compasses in the right direction. Nonetheless, to maximize these school-based efforts, other adults who work regularly with adolescents should be aware of the potentially harmful effects of cultural narcissism, especially as these adults try to refine the moral systems of the young people under their care.

Adults working with adolescent groups such as the Girl Scouts and the Boy Scouts may find their organizations particularly suited for nurturing prosocial conduct and character development. For example, presently existing scout codes tend, directly and indirectly, to emphasize the personal and social benefits of practicing the moral sentiments of sympathy, fairness, duty, and self-control. These sentiments are further reinforced by various merit badges, such as "Citizenship in the Community" and "Citizenship in the Nation" (*Boy Scout Requirements*, 1999, pp. 44–46), which, at their core, are based upon several of Wilson's (1998) sentiments. Other merit badges, as well as structured progression through scout rank (e.g., Second-Class Scout, First-Class Scout, etc.), require activities that derive from various moral sentiments and that provide youngsters additional contexts for refining their self-understanding, social cognition, and moral judgment (Whitacre, 1998).

Recreation leaders in municipal playgrounds and counselors in summer camps are also in positions to foster the moral system of young people, while diluting the influence of cultural narcissism. For instance, in structuring play activities for young children, these leaders should stress teamwork, cooperation, and fairness. And with activities requiring some sort of "clean-up" (e.g., putting away glue, paper, string, etc.), all children should be held responsible for contributing efficiently and collaboratively. With adolescents who are involved with more formal games (e.g., sandlot baseball and playground basketball leagues), recreation leaders, in overseeing these activities and perhaps acting as referees or umpires, should stress among the players the need for fairness, responsibility, duty, and self-control. These personal attributes should be emphasized while the children are playing in these games and while they are "closing down" the playground afterwards (e.g., returning equipment to appropriate places, removing soda cans and bottles, etc.). Supervising adolescent athletics, as well as monitoring the play behavior among younger children, provides recreation leaders further opportunities to dilute the surge of cultural narcissism by challenging a young person's sense of entitlement (e.g., the adolescent who always must win regardless of the cost to self and others) and by checking the youngster's feelings of grandiosity (e.g., the adolescent who refuses to play cooperatively because of a sense of superiority).

Teachers, scout leaders, recreation supervisors, and camp counselors can contribute dramatically to the enrichment of a young person's moral system, including the prosocial conduct and character development that derive from and interpenetrate this system. Yet the primary responsibility for guiding these developments resides with the parents. As primary caregivers, parents provide the initial social stimulation and environment that enhances the child's self-understanding and social cognition. Through modeling, anecdotes, and admonishment, parents also stimulate their child's moral sentiments and provide their child prescriptive and pro-scriptive blueprints for making moral judgments. Building on these pro-cesses, Baumrind (1973), in her now-classic study of child-rearing prac-tices, argued that most parents ideally want their child to display a cluster of traits she called *instrumental competence*: social responsibility, inde-pendence, achievement orientation, and vitality (p. 4). Upon close exami-nation, it is clear that each of these traits involves refinements in self-understanding and social cognition. Furthermore, Baumrind claimed that child-rearing practices which stressed parental control, clarity of parent-child communication, maturity demands, and nurturance would generally lead to higher levels of instrumental competence. These practices like-wise have the potential of appealing to the child's moral sentiments (e.g., duty and self-control), while once again providing situations for under-standing the self and others.

A parent who is sensitive to the influence of the culture of narcissism, particularly as it magnifies the normal narcissism of adolescence, may countervail such narcissism directly by underscoring the importance of control and maturity demands as a balance to entitlement and grandios-ity; yet, the parent must do so with clear communication and understand-ing so that the teenager's potential feelings of resentment are mollified. In contrast, a narcissistic household, where the parents themselves are torch-bearers of grandiosity, entitlement, self-absorption, and devaluation of others, could abet the construction of narcissistic personalities in the chil-dren. A similar effect on children and adolescents might be traced to recreation and scouting officials whose belief systems and self-lifeplans have been considerably influenced by the culture of narcissism, despite the prosocial assumptions allegedly embedded in their respective organi-zations and institutions.

Peer Influence

Although parents and other adults do influence a child's and adolescent's belief system and conduct, research has challenged the domination of the adult role within this formative process. In *The Nurture Assumption: Why Children Turn Out the Way They Do* (1998), Harris suggested that children's experiences outside the home in the company of their peers influence them the most. If Harris is correct in claiming that children socialize children, and if the narcissistic perspective dominates the adolescent subculture that is the socializing agent, then children entering adolescence would be clearly at risk. Despite parental efforts to provide their children some sense of balance to the more alluring elements of cultural narcissism, the influence of the peer may override these efforts and accentuate the incipient exhibitions of normal narcissism that almost all adolescents display in some form (see chapter 3 for a full account of this process). Especially disquieting is that such peer influence, in encouraging flagrant displays of grandiosity, entitlement, and devaluation of others, could posit the seeds of violence. As Bushman and Baumeister (1998) have demonstrated, when narcissistic personalities are challenged or thwarted (as might occur when a classroom teacher disciplines a narcissistic teenager, or when another youth contradicts or crosses a narcissistic peer), violent behavior could result. In the larger context of our argument, teachers striving to nurture such a student's moral system would most probably become frustrated, and this would be most obvious in classrooms where peers are encouraging one another's narcissistic behavior.

Final Considerations: Scientific Investigation of the Emotional Brain and the Moral Sentiments

Research conducted on the brain throughout the 1990s emphasized that cognition and emotion are inextricably woven together, with thought processes wired to feeling and emotions wired to thinking (Damasio, 1994; LeDoux, 1996). One of the conclusions of this research was that reason and emotion should be harmonized as, together, they provide the light and heat that helps humans negotiate personal understanding and social interaction. In several ways, this new paradigm replaces the earlier belief in which emotion was viewed as a saboteur of reason and as an irrational component of the human condition that blinds logic and judgment. This is not to suggest that emotion cannot cloud thinking, a reality that is captured by the adage that "I was so upset that I could not think straight." Rather, emotion should be monitored in such a way that it becomes balanced with and contributes to reason and judgment.

In *Emotional Intelligence* (1995), Goleman introduced the notion of "metamood," a process whereby a person practices the skill of standing back from one's emotions and reflecting upon whether the emotion in question (e.g., anger) is appropriate, reasonably displayed, and justified. Commenting on this type of reflection, Goleman (1995) cited Aristotle's *Nicomachean Ethics*: "Anyone can become angry—that is easy. But to be angry with the right person, to the right degree, at the right time, for the right purpose, and in the right way—that is not easy" (p. ix). Underpinning the crux of Aristotle's observations, metamood is the emotional counterpart to "metacognition," the term used to describe an awareness of one's thought processes (Goleman, 1995, p. 46). In the context of social interaction, metamood is an essential skill for it helps prevent an "emotional hijacking" (Goleman, 1995, p. 14). As Goleman explained this event:

> At those moments, evidence suggests, a center of the limbic brain proclaims an emergency, recruiting the rest of the brain into its urgent agenda. The hijacking occurs in an instant, triggering this reaction crucial moments before the neocortex, the thinking brain, has had a chance to glimpse fully what is happening, let alone decide if it is a good idea. The hallmark of such a hijack is that once the moment passes, those so possessed have the sense of not knowing what came over them. (p. 14)

Emotional hijackings are part of the human experience; however, because of the emotional whirlwind during adolescence, it is predictable that high schoolers are frequently the victims of such hijackings. Teachers, and particularly high school disciplinarians, can attest to the many demerits given to students for fighting or for verbal altercations because one student perceived that she was "disrespected" by another as the two eyed each other in the school cafeteria. There may not have been any intent to the glance on the part of the alleged perpetrating student, but the other teenager, caught up in the emotion of perhaps just a "bad day," believed otherwise, with the brief locking of retinas leading to insults and even fists.

To correct such "emotional illiteracy," Goleman (1995) suggested that teachers have students practice a problem-solving model called Situation, Options, Consequence, Solutions (SOCS), an acronym for a four-step process developed by Tim Shriver, director of the social competence program in the New Haven Connecticut schools. In applying these steps, students "say what the situation is and how it makes you feel; think about your options for solving the problems and what the consequences might be; pick a solution and execute it" (Goleman, 1995, p. 281). This approach would clearly provide practice of metamood, which in turn would enhance self-understanding and social cognition. However, teachers should monitor student metamood so that it does not become obsessive and contribute to a narcissistic student's sense of self-absorption. Equally important, the SOCS method, executed correctly, is ultimately social, guiding students to mentally trace the impact of their decisions on others. Once again, this dimension of the process, operationalized appropriately by the teacher, can undercut the forces of cultural narcissism that may prompt narcissistic students to select solutions that might gratify the self and devalue others.

Besides emphasizing the integrated nature of thought and feeling, research on the emotional brain has also contributed to a fuller understanding of the moral sentiments as such feeling states influence prosocial conduct and moral action. While such efforts have not yet yielded palpable results that would impact directly on the overall moral system, Edward Wilson (1998), not to be confused with James Wilson, the author of the moral sentiments, has been at the vanguard of these initiatives. He maintained that ethics, as expressed as a code of principles, is "driven by hereditary dispositions in mental development, the 'moral sentiments' of Enlightenment philosophers, causing broad convergence across cultures, while reaching precise form in each culture according to historical circumstance" (Wilson, 1998, p. 262). Developing these points further, Wilson noted that "[t]he sentiments are thus derived from epigenetic rules, hereditary biases in mental development . . . that influence concepts and decisions made from them. The primary origin of the moral instincts is the dynamic relation between cooperation and defection" (1998, p. 275).

From here, Wilson examined how cooperation and defection operated in early civilizations, with cooperative humans generally surviving longer and producing more offspring. "It is to be expected that in the course of evolutionary history, genes predisposing people toward cooperative behavior would have come to dominate in the human population as a whole" (1998, p. 276). Wilson concluded that a detailed analysis of the moral sentiments, using the tools of biology, physiology, and psychology, would provide rich dividends in understanding how ethical behavior operates. He offered a convergent approach grounded in the following strategies, which are quoted directly:

- *The definition of the moral sentiments*: first by precise descriptions from experimental psychology, then by analysis of the underlying neural and endocrine responses.

- *The genetics of the moral sentiments*: most easily approached through measurements of the heritability of the psychological and physiological processes of ethical behavior, and eventually, with difficulty, by identification of the prescribing gene.
- *The development of the moral sentiments as products of genes and environment.* The research is most effective when conducted on two levels: the histories of ethical systems as part of the emergence of different cultures, and the cognitive development of individuals living in a variety of cultures. Such investigations are already well along in anthropology and psychology. In the future they will be augmented by contributions from biology.
- *The deep history of the moral sentiments*: why they exist in the first place, presumably by their contributions to survival and reproductive success during the long periods of prehistoric time in which they genetically evolved. (Wilson, 1998, p. 279)

Such research appears significant and profound, providing a close window into the workings of the emotional and moral brain. Yet this research program would clearly not be without controversy, with implications that would be both social and ethical. For instance, would people be singled out as having inadequate "moral genes"? Would these people be barred from marriage, and from certain jobs and professions? Would they have their genetic moral shortcomings made public and medically corrected? Would parents, teachers, and physicians be partners in constructing individual education programs for students that included some sort of genetic moral engineering? Who would monitor this process?

Despite these disquieting, ethical challenges, Wilson's 1998 research paradigm is significant because it verifies once again the powerful function of the moral sense in nurturing moral awareness and ethical conduct. Relating to this awareness, the activities in the Praxis chapters were designed to refine all components of the moral system. However, the unique blending of idea and product technology has been especially formatted to excite the moral sentiments through animating and magnifying the ethical dimensions embedded throughout the English, social studies, mathematics, and science curricula. And finally, this blending of idea and product technology is intended to reveal the potentially negative effects of cultural narcissism that, in luring adolescents from prosocial behavior, entices so many of them to drown in the clear pool of self-absorption, entitlement, and grandiosity.

References

Allen, D., & Ryan, K. (1969). *Microteaching.* Reading, MA: Addison-Wesley.

American Association for the Advancement of Science. (1993). *Benchmarks for science literacy.* New York: Oxford University Press.

Antes, R.L., & Norton, M.L. (1994). Another view of school reform: Values and ethics restored. *Counseling and Values, 38*, 215–222.

Applebee, A. N. (1992, September). Stability and change in the high school canon. *English Journal, 81*(5), 27–32.

Armstrong, T. (1994). *Multiple intelligences in the classroom.* Alexandria. VA: Association for Supervision and Curriculum Development.

Baldwin, J. (1902). *Social and ethical interpretations in mental development* (3rd ed.). New York: McGraw-Hill.

Bambara, T. (1993). A girl's story. In J. Loughery (Ed.), *First sightings: Stories of American youth* (pp. 130–141). New York: Persea Books.

Baumrind, D. (1973). The development of instrumental competence through socialization. In A.D. Pick. (Ed.), *Minnesota Symposium on Child Psychology* (Vol. 7). Minneapolis: University of Minnesota Press.

Beach, R., & Marshall, J. (1991). *Teaching literature in the secondary school.* New York: Harcourt Brace Jovanovich.

Behrmann, M. (1998). Assistive technology for young children in special education. In C. Dede (Ed.), *Association for Supervision and Curriculum Development Yearbook, 1998* (pp. 73–91). Alexandria, VA: Association for Supervision and Curriculum Development.

Bennett, W. (1992). *The devaluing of America: The fight for our culture and our children.* New York: Touchstone.

Bennigna, J. (1988). An emerging synthesis in moral education. *Phi Delta Kappan,* 69 (February): 415–418.

Berman, J. (1990). *Narcissism and the novel.* New York: NYU Press.

Biehler, F., & Snowman, J. (1993). *Psychology applied to teaching* (7th ed.). Boston: Houghton Mifflin.

Bitter, G. G., & Pierson, M. E. (1999). *Using Technology in the Classroom* (4th ed.). Needham Heights, MA: Allyn & Bacon.

Bloom, B. S., Engelhart, M. S., Frost, E. J., Hill, W. H., & Krathwohl, D. R. (1956). *Taxonomy of educational objectives. Handbook I: Cognitive domain.* New York: McKay.

Bowles, S., & Gintis, H. (1976). *Schooling in capitalist America.* New York: Basic Books.

Boy Scout Requirements. (1999). Irving, TX: Boy Scouts of America.

Boyer, B., & Semrau, P. (1995, January/February). A constructionist approach to social studies: Integrating technology. *Technology and Social Studies, 7*(3), 14–16.

Branagh, K., & Ritstein, D. (Co-directors). (1996). *Hamlet* [videocassette]. (Available from Columbia/Tristar Studio)

Brown, K. (1993, April/May). Video production in the classroom: Creating successes for students and schools. *TechTrends,* 32–35.

Brown Yoder, M. (1999, April). The student WebQuest. *Learning & Leading with technology,* 6–9; 52–53.

Burke, J. (1999). *The English teacher's companion: A complete guide to classroom, curriculum, and the profession.* Portsmouth, NH: Boynton/Cook.

Burstyn, J. (1984). *Victorian education and the ideal of womanhood.* New Brunswick, NJ: Rutgers University Press.

Bushman, B., & Baumeister, R. (1998). Threatened egotism, narcissism, self-esteem, and direct displacement: Does self-love or self-hate lead to violence? *Journal of Personality and Social Psychology, 75*(1), 219–228.

Cairney, W. J, Cassel, J. F., Cully, P., Girard, J. C., Rainis, K. G., Uno, G. E., & Ward, L. K. (1998). *BSCS biology: An ecological approach* (8th ed.). [Green version, teacher's edition]. Dubuque, IA: Kendall Hunt.

Campbell, L., Campbell, B., & Dickenson, D. (1996). *Teaching and learning through multiple intelligences.* Needham Heights, MA: Allyn & Bacon.

Cartopedia: The ultimate world reference atlas. (1995). [CD-ROM]. New York: Dorling Kindersley Multimedia.

CBS News [On-line]. *Testimony on gene therapy deaths.* Retrieved February 6, 2000, from the World Wide Web: .cbs.com/now/story/ 0,1597,156168–412,00.shtml

Chapin, H. (1988). Cat's in the Cradle. On *Greatest Stories Live* [audio CD]. Wea/Elektra Entertainment.

Chazan, B. (1985). *Contemporary approaches to moral education: Analyzing alternative theories.* New York: Teachers College Press.

Chiappetta, E. L., Koballa, Jr., T. R., & Collette, A. (1998). *Science instruction in the middle and secondary schools* (4th ed.). Upper Saddle River, NJ: Prentice-Hall.

Chopin, K. (1981). The story of an hour. In M. Ferguson (Ed.), *Images of women in literature* (3rd ed., pp. 395–397). Boston: Houghton Mifflin.

Cloning: How and why. (1998). [videocassette] Madison, WI: Hawkhill Associates.

Coles, R. (1997). *The moral intelligence of children.* New York: Random House.

Commager, H. (Ed.). (1962). *Noah Webster's American spelling book.* New York: Teachers College Press.

Copley, J. S. (1773). *Mr. and Mrs. Mifflin.* [portrait]. Philadelphia Museum of Art.

Copley, J. S. (1776). *Copley Family.* [portrait]. Washington, DC: National Gallery.

Craig, R. (1994, May/June). Self-interest and moral imagination: A way of teaching social justice. *The Social Studies, 85*(3), 127–129.

Cremin, L. (Ed.). (1957). *The republic and the school: Horace Mann on the education of free man.* New York: Teachers College Press.

Cremin, L. (1964). *The transformation of the school: Progressivism in American education, 1876–1957.* New York: Vintage Books.

Cremin, L. (1970). *American education: The colonial experience, 1607–1783.* New York: Harper Books.

Damasio, A. (1994). *Descarte's error: Emotion, reason, and the human brain.* New York: Grosset/Putnam.

Damon, W. (1983). *Social and personality development: Infancy through adolescence.* New York: Norton.

Damon, W. (1988). *The moral child: Nurturing children's natural moral growth.* New York: Free Press.

Damon, W. (1995). *Greater expectations: Overcoming the culture of indulgence in America's homes and schools.* New York: Free Press.

Daniels, R. (1991). *Coming to America: A history of immigration and ethnicity in American life.* New York: Harper-Collins.

Daniels, R. (1997). *Not like us: Immigrants and minorities in modern America, 1890–1924.* Chicago: Ivan R. Dee.

D'Arcangelo, M. (Project Manager and Producer). (1997). *Exploring our multiple intelligences* [CD-ROM]. Alexandria, VA: Association for Supervision and Curriculum Development. Stock # 59276.

Dewey, J. (1916). *Democracy and education.* New York: Macmillan.

Dewey, J. (1976). *The school and society.* (Jo Ann Boydston, Ed). Carbondale, IL: Southern Illinois University Press. (Original work published 1899)

Dickinson, E. (1959). I'm nobody! Who are you? In R. Linscott (Ed.), *Selected poems and letters of Emily Dickinson* (p. 75). New York: Doubleday Anchor Books.

Dockterman, D. (1988). *The decisions, decisions guide to critical thinking in the classroom* [computer software manual]. Cambridge, MA: Tom Snyder Productions.

Dockterman, D. (1990). *Decisions, decisions: The environment* [computer software]. Cambridge, MA. Tom Snyder Productions.

Dodge, B. (site visited 7-5-99). *The WebQuest Page* [on-line], available: http://edweb.sdsu-edu/webquest/webquest.html

Dunphy, D. (1963). The social structure of urban adolescent peer groups. *Sociometry, 26,* 230–246.

Dusick, Diane M. (1998, Autumn/Winter). The learning effectiveness of educational technology: What does that really mean? *Educational Technology Review,* 10–12.

Dyrli, O. E. (1993, October). The internet: Bringing resources to the classroom. *Technology & Learning,* 50–58.

Edwards, C. H. (1993). *Classroom discipline and management.* New York: Macmillan.

Eggen, P., & Kauchak, D. (1992). *Educational psychology: Classroom connections.* New York: Macmillan.

Elkind, D. (1984). *All grown up & no place to go: Teenagers in crisis.* Reading, MA: Addison-Wesley.

Emde, R., Biringen, Z., Clyman, R., & Oppenheim, D. (1991). The moral self of infancy: Affective core and procedural knowledge. *Developmental Review, 11,* 251–270.

Encarta: Virtual Globe 99. (1993–98). [CD-ROM]. Microsoft Corporation.

English, P. W. (1995). *Geography: People and places in a changing world.* St. Paul, MN: West.

Erikson, E. (1963). *Childhood and society* (35th anniversary ed.). New York: Norton.

Erikson, E. (1968). *Identity: Youth and crisis.* New York: Harper & Row.

Faragher, J., Buhle, M., & Czitrom, S. (1994). *Out of many: A history of the American people.* Englewood Cliffs, NJ: Prentice Hall.

Feke, R. (1741). *Isaac Royal and family.* [portrait]. Harvard University Law School Art Gallery.

Ford, P. L. (Ed.) (1962). *The New England primer.* New York: Teachers College Press. (Original work published 1897)

Froyen, L. A., & Iverson, A. M. (1999). *Schoolwide and classroom management* (3rd ed.). Upper Saddle River, NJ: Prentice-Hall.

Gallagher, J. M., & Reid, D. K. (1981). *The learning theory of Piaget & Inhelder.* Belmont, CA: Brook/Cole.

Gardner, H. (1983). *Frames of mind: The theory of multiple intelligences.* New York: Basic Books.

Gardner, H. (1991). *The unschooled mind: How children think and how schools should teach.* New York: Basic Books.

Gardner, H. (1993). *Multiple intelligences: The theory in practice.* New York: Basic Books.

Gardner, H. (1995, November). Reflections on multiple intelligences: Myths and messages. *Phi Delta Kappan,* 200–203; 206–209.

Gardner, H. (1999). *Intelligence reframed: Multiple intelligences for the 21ˢᵗ century.* New York: Basic Books.

Garrity, J. (1994). *The story of America.* New York: Holt, Rinehart, and Winston.

Gilligan, C. (1982). *In a different voice: Psychological theory and women's development.* Cambridge, MA: Harvard University Press.

Gleason, P. (1992). *Speaking of diversity: Language and diversity in twentieth-century America.* Baltimore, MD: Johns Hopkins University Press.

Goldberg, C. (1980). *In defense of narcissism: The creative self in search of meaning.* New York: Gardner Press.

Goleman, D. (1995). *Emotional intelligence.* New York: Bantam Books.

Good, T., & Brophy, J. (1990). *Educational psychology: A realistic approach* (4ᵗʰ ed.). New York: Longman Press.

Grabe, M., & Grabe, C. (1998). *Learning with internet tools: A primer.* Boston: Houghton Mifflin Company.

Grant, C. A. (1994, Winter). Challenging the myths about multicultural education. *Multicultural Education,* 4–9.

Gray, R., & Herrick, M. A. (1995, November/December). Technology and multicultural education. *TechTrends,* 32–33.

Gregorc, A. F. (1985). *Inside styles: Beyond the basics.* Columbia, CT: Gregorc Associates.

Greven, P. (1990). *Spare the child: The religious roots of punishment and the psychological impact of physical abuse.* New York: Knopf.

Guild, P. B., & Garger, S. (1998). *Marching to different drummers* (2nd ed.). Alexandria, VA: Association for Supervision and Curriculum Development.

Hamilton, A. (1999, March 15). Next on the net: Pirated movies. *Time,* 73.

Hancock, V. (1996, December). Information literacy and the technology revolution: Implications from research for teaching and learning. *TIE Newsletter (11)* 2; 4–5; 17–18.

Harris, J. (1995, May). Educational telecomputing activities: Problem-solving projects. *Learning and Leading With Technology, 22*(8), 59–63.

Harris, J. (1995). Where is the child's environment? A group socialization theory of development. *Psychological Review, 102*(3), 468–489.

Harris, J. (1998). *Design tools for the internet-supported classroom.* Alexandria, VA: Association for Supervision and Curriculum Development.

Harris, J. R. (1998). *The nurture assumption: Why children turn out the way they do.* New York: Touchstone.

Heinich, R., Molenda, M., Russell, J., & Smaldino, S. (1999). *Instructional media and technologies for learning* (6th ed.). Upper Saddle River, NJ: Merrill.

Heller, K. (1998, May 3). On being, not nothingness. *The Philadelphia Inquirer,* p. F1.

Hofstetter, F. T. (1994, Winter). Is multimedia the next literacy? *Educators Tech Exchange,* 6–13.

Hooper, S., & Rieber, L. P. (1995). Teaching with technology. In A. Ornstein (Ed.), *Teaching: Theory into practice* (pp. 154–170). Needham Heights, MA: Allyn & Bacon.

Howard, R. (Director). (1999). *Edtv* [videotape]. Universal Pictures.

Hubley, J. (Director/Producer). (1975). *Everybody Rides the Carousel* [videocassette]. (Available from Amazon.com. <http://amazon.com>)

Hughes, F., & Noppe, L. (1991). *Human development across the lifespan.* New York: Macmillan.

Hutchins, W. J. (1917). *Children's code of morals for elementary schools.* Washington, DC: Character Education Institute.

Hyerle, D. (1996). *Visual tools for constructing knowledge.* Alexandria, VA: Association for Supervision and Curriculum Development.

HyperStudio. (1993–98). [CD-ROM]. Lel Cajon, CA: Roger Wagner Publishing.

Inspiration. (1988–98). [CD-ROM]. Portland, OR: Inspiration Software.

Inspiration. [review of the computer software program *Inspiration*]. (1999, August). *Technology & Learning, 20,* 45.

International Society for Technology in Education. (2000). *National educational technology standards for students: Connecting curriculum and technology.* Eugene, OR: International Society for Technology in Education.

Johnson, D., & Johnson, R. (1991). *Learning together and alone: Cooperation, competition, and individualistic learning* (3rd ed.). Englewood Cliffs, NJ: Prentice-Hall.

Kaestle, C. (1983). *Pillars of the republic: Common schools and American society.* New York: Hill & Wang.

Kagan, J. (1984). *The nature of the child.* New York: Basic Books.

Kagan, J. (1994). *The nature of the child* (anniversary ed.). New York: Basic Books.

Kasman Valenza, J. (2000, January 13). Students and teachers alike can benefit from rubrics. *Philadelphia Inquirer,* p. F5.

Katz, L. (1993). All about me: Are we developing our children's self-esteem or their narcissism? *American Educator, 17*(2), 18–23.

Keller, M., & Edelstein, W. (1993). The development of the moral sense from childhood to adolescence. In G. Noam and T. Wren (Eds.), *The moral self* (pp. 310–336). Cambridge, MA: MIT Press.

Kernberg, O. (1975). *Borderline conditions and pathological narcissism.* New York: Jason Aronson.

Kilpatrick, W. (1992). *Why Johnny can't tell right from wrong*. New York: Simon & Schuster.

Kindsvatter, R., Wilen, W., & Ishler, M. (1992). *Dynamics of effective teaching* (2nd ed.). New York: Longman.

Kindsvatter, R., Wilen, W., & Ishler, M. (1996). *Dynamics of effective teaching* (3rd ed.). New York: Longman.

Kohlberg, L. (1970). Education for justice: A modern statement of the platonic view. *Moral Education—Five Lectures*. Cambridge, MA: Harvard University Press.

Kohn, A. (1990). *The brighter side of human nature*. New York: Basic Books.

Kohn, A. (1997). How not to teach values: A critical look at character education. *Phi Delta Kappan, 78*(6), 429–439.

Kohut, H. (1971). *The analysis of self*. New York: International Universities Press.

Lasch, C. (1979). *The culture of narcissism: American life in an age of diminishing expectations*. New York: Norton.

Latham, A. (1999, February). Computers and achievement. *Educational Leadership, 56*(5), 87–88.

LeDoux, J. (1996). *The emotional brain: The mysterious underpinnings of emotional life*. New York: Touchstone.

Leming, J. S. (1993). In search of effective character education. *Educational Leadership, 51*, 63–71.

Lewis, M., & Brooks-Gunn, J. (1979). *Social cognition and the acquisition of self*. New York, NY: Plenum Press.

Lickona, T. (1983). *Raising good children from birth through the teenage years: How to help your child develop a lifelong sense of honesty, decency, and respect for others*. New York: Bantam.

Lickona, T. (1988, February). Four strategies for fostering character development in children. *Phi Delta Kappan, 69*(6), 419–423.

Lickona, T. (1991). *Educating for character: How our schools can teach respect and responsibility*. New York: Bantam.

Lickona, T. (1995). A comprehensive approach to character education. In D. E. Eberly (Ed.), *The content of America's character: Recovering civic virtue* (pp. 141–161). Lantham, NY: Madison Books.

Lockwood, A. M. (1997). *Character education: Controversy and consensus.* Thousand Oaks, CA: Corwin Press.

Lovell, D. (Producer), & Zeffirelli, F. (Director). (1990). *Hamlet* [videodisc]. (Available from Warner Home Video, 4000 Warner Blvd., Burbank, CA 91522)

Marcia, J. (1980). Identity in adolescence. In J. Adelson (Ed.). *Handbook of adolescent psychology.* New York: Wiley.

Marzano, R., Pickering, D., & McTighe, J. (1993). *Assessing student outcomes: Performance assessment using the dimensions of learning model.* Alexandria, VA: Association for Supervision and Curriculum Development.

Masterman, J. (1981). *The narcissistic and borderline disorders: An integrated developmental approach.* New York: Brunner/Mazel.

Matthews, B. E., & Riley, C. K. (1995). Teaching and evaluating outdoor ethics programs. Vienna, VA: National Wildlife Federation (ERIC Document Reproduction Services No: ED 401 097).

McCarthy, B. (1987). *The 4MAT system: Teaching to learning styles with right/left mode techniques.* Barrington, IL: EXCEL.

McClellan, B. E. (1992). *Schools and the shaping of character: Moral education in America, 1607–present.* Bloomington, IN: ERIC Clearinghouse for Social Studies/Social Science Education and the Social Studies Development Center.

McDaniel, A. (1998). Character education: Developing effective programs. *Journal of Extension, 36* (2), 1–10.

McGinniss, D. (1985). *When children don't learn: Understanding the biology and psychology of learning disabilities.* New York: Basic Books.

McGrath, B. (1998). Partners in learning: Twelve ways technology changes the teacher-student relationship. *T.H.E. Journal,* 58–61.

McNeil, J. (1995). *Curriculum: The teachers' initiative.* Englewood Cliffs, NJ: Prentice-Hall.

McNiff, W. (1969). *The pageant of literature: Greek and Roman writers.* New York: Macmillan.

Mead, G. (1934). *Mind, self, and society from the standpoint of a social behaviorist.* Chicago, IL: University of Chicago Press.

Mehlinger, H. D. (1995). *School reform in the information age.* Bloomington, IN: Center for Excellence in Education.

Mehlinger, H. D. (1996). School reform in the information age. *Phi Delta Kappan,* 400–407.

Mills, S. (1994, January/February). Integrated learning systems: New technology for classrooms of the future. *TechTrends,* 27–28; 31.

Milone, M. (1995). Electronic portfolios: Who's doing them and how? *Technology & Learning,* 28–29; 32; 36.

Mitchell, J. (1992). *Adolescent struggle for selfhood and identity.* Calgary, Alberta: Detselig Enterprise.

National Council of Teachers of English, International Reading Association. (1996). *Standards of the English Language Arts.* Urbana, IL: National Council of Teachers of English.

National Council of Teachers of Mathematics. (1989). *Curriculum and evaluation standards for school mathematics.* Reston, VA: National Council of Teachers of Mathematics.

National Research Council. [On-line]. *National science education standards.* Retrieved February 3, 2000, from the World Wide Web: http://books.nap.edu/html/nseas/html/6a.html#changing

Nelson, G. M. [On-line]. Teaching bioethics. In *Access excellence: Classrooms of the 21st century.* Retrieved February 3, 2000, from the World Wide Web: http://accessexcellence.org/21st/TL/TBE

Nyberg, D., & Egan, K. (1981). *The erosion of education: Socialization and the schools.* New York: Teachers College Press.

Ogle, D. M. (1989). The know, want to know, learn strategy. In K. D. Muth (Ed.), *Children's comprehension of text* (pp. 205–223). Newark, DE: International Reading Association.

Orwig, A. (1995, September). Bridging the ages with help from technology. *Technology & Learning,* 26; 28–29; 32–33.

Pangle, L., & Pangle, T. (1993). *The learning of liberty: The educational ideas of the American founders.* Lawrence, KS: University of Kansas Press.

Peck, K. L., & Dorricott, D. (1994, April). Why use technology? *Educational Leadership*, 11–14.

Peha, J. M. (1995, October). How K-12 teachers are using computer networks. *Educational Leadership*, 18–25.

Piaget, J. (1965). *The moral judgment of the child.* New York: The Free Press.

Piaget, J., & Inhelder, B. (1969). *The psychology of the child.* New York: Basic Books.

Pitts, L. (1998, July 18). The monstrosity of baby killing may be rooted in our national culture of brattiness. *The Philadelphia Inquirer*, p. A12.

Pollack, W. (1998). *Real boys: Rescuing our sons from the myth of boyhood.* New York: Random House.

Posamentier, A. S., & Stepelman, J. (1999). *Teaching secondary school mathematics* (5th ed.). Upper Saddle River, NJ: Merrill.

PowerPoint. (1995). In Microsoft Office. [CD-ROM]. Microsoft Corporation.

Rose, D. H., & Meyer, A. (1994, April). The role of technology in language arts instruction. *Language Arts, 71*, 290–294.

Rosenblatt, L. (1968). *Literature as exploration* (rev. ed.). New York: Noble and Noble, Publishers.

Rothstein, A. (1980). *The narcissistic pursuit of perfection.* New York: International Universities Press.

Rush, B. (1965). Thoughts upon the mode of education proper in a republic. In F. Rudolph (Ed.), *Essays on education in the early republic* (pp. 9–23). Cambridge, MA: Harvard University Press.

Ryan, F. (1985). *Lasch and the portrayal of narcissistic personality in adolescent fiction.* Unpublished doctoral dissertation, Temple University, Philadelphia, PA.

Ryan, F. (1993). The perils of multiculturalism: Schooling for the group. *Educational Horizons, 71*, 134–138.

Ryan, F. (1996). Unmasking the face of narcissism: A prerequisite for moral education. *Journal of Educational Thought, 30*(2), 159–170.

Ryan, F. (1997). Narcissism and the moral sense: Moral education in the secondary sociology classroom. *The Social Studies, 88*(5), 233–237.

Ryan, F., Bednar, M., & Sweeder, J. (1999). Technology, narcissism, and the moral sense: Implications for instruction. *British Journal of Educational Technology, 30*(2), 115–128.

Ryan, K. (1986). The new moral education. *Phi Delta Kappan, 68* (November), 228–283.

Ryan, K., & Bohlin, K. (1999). *Building character in schools: Practical ways to bring moral instruction to life.* San Francisco: Jossey-Bass.

Schwarz, M., & O'Connor, J. (1998). *Exploring a changing world.* New York: Globe.

Selman, R. (1980). *The growth of interpersonal understanding.* New York: Academic Press.

Sennett, R. (1974). *The fall of public man: On the social psychology of capitalism.* New York: Vintage Books.

Shaffer, D. (1994). *Social and personality development* (3rd ed.). Pacific Grove, CA: Brooks/Cole.

Shakespeare Interactive: Hamlet, Prince of Denmark. (1996). [CD-ROM]. Available from Sante Fe New Media. New York: G.K. Hall & Co./Macmillan Library Reference/Simon & Schuster.

Shakespeare, W. (1957). *The tragedy of Hamlet: Prince of Denmark.* Baltimore, MD: Penguin.

Shakespeare, W. (1964). *Romeo and Juliet.* New York, NY: Signet.

Sherman, M. (1991). *Videographing the pictorial sequence.* Washington, DC: Association for Educational Communications and Technology.

Simon, S., Howe, L., & Kirschenbaum, H. (1972). Values clarification: A handbook of practical strategies for teachers and students. New York: Hart.

Simpson, D., & Bruckheimer, J. (Producers), & Smith, J. (Director). (1995). *Dangerous minds* [videocassette]. (Available from Buena Vista Home Video, Dept. CS, Burbank, CA 91521)

Smetana, J. (1989). Toddler's social interactions in the context of moral and conventional transgressions in the home. *Developmental Psychology, 25*(4), 499–508.

Smibert, J. (1729). *Dean George Berkeley and his family.* [portrait]. Yale University Art Gallery.

Smith, D. (1995, November). Moral teaching in geography. *Journal of Geography in Higher Education, 19*(3), 271–283.

Sommers, C. (1984, Summer). Ethics without virtue: Moral education in America. *American Scholar, 53*, 381–389.

Sowell, T. (1981). *Ethnic America: A history.* New York: Basic Books.

Spring, J. (1986). *The American school, 1642–1985.* New York: Longman.

Sroufe, L., Cooper, R., & DeHart, G. (1996). *Child development: Its nature and course* (3rd ed.). New York: McGraw-Hill.

Stonebarger, B. *The human genome project.* (1999). [videocassette]. Madison, WI: Hawkhill Associates.

Sugarman, S. (1976). *Sin and madness: Studies in narcissism.* Philadelphia, PA: Westminster Press.

Sweeder, J. (1996). Helping classroom teachers construct rationales for infusing technology into classroom instruction. In D. Carey, R. Carey, D. A. Willis, & J. Willis (Eds.), *Technology and Teacher Education Annual, 1996.* Charlottesville, VA: Association for the Advancement of Computing in Education.

Sykes, C. (1995). *Dumbing down our kids: Why American children feel good about themselves but can't read, write, or add.* New York: St. Martin's Press.

Sylwester, R. (1994, October). How emotions affect learning. *Educational Leadership, 52*(2), 60–65.

Takaki, R. (1993). *A different mirror: History of multicultural America.* Boston: Little, Brown.

Tanner, L. (1997). *Dewey's laboratory school: Lessons for today.* New York: Teachers College Press.

Tapscott, D. (1998). *Growing up digital: The rise of the net generation.* New York: McGraw-Hill.

The multicultural peoples of North America. (1993). [video series]. Bala Cynwyd, PA: Schlessinger Video Productions.

Tompkins, J. (Ed.). (1980). *Reader-response criticism from formalism to post-structuralism.* Baltimore: Johns Hopkins University Press.

Van Hoose, J. (1980). The impact of television usage on emerging adolescents. *High School Journal, 63*(6), 239–243.

Vocational, Technical, and Adult Education, Incorporated [VTAE]. (1993). *Using interactive videodisc technology to teach mathematics and electronics* [videotape]. (Available from Wisconsin Foundation for Vocational, Technical, and Adult Education, Incorporated, One Foundation Circle, Waunakee, WI, 53597–8914)

Vygotsky, L. (1976). Play and its role in development and evolution. In J. Bruner, A. Jolly, & K. Sylva (Eds.), *Play: Its role in development in evolution* (pp. 537–554). New York: Basic Books.

Warfel, H. (1936). *Noah Webster: Schoolmaster to America.* New York: Macmillan.

Weiner, J. (1998, May 10). Should you really let these people into your house? *The Philadelphia Inquirer,* p. F10.

Whitacre, E. (Ed.). (1998). *The boy scout handbook* (11th ed.). Irving, TX: Boy Scouts of America.

Wilson, E. (1998). *Consilience: The unity of knowledge.* New York: Random House.

Wilson, J. Q. (1993). *The moral sense.* New York: Free Press.

Woolfolk, A. E. (1998). *Educational psychology* (7th ed.). Needham Heights, MA: Allyn & Bacon.

Wright, W. (1980). Teaching writing in the age of narcissism. *English Journal, 69*(8), 26–29.

Wynne, E. (1985–86, December/January). The great tradition in education: Transmitting moral values. *Educational Leadership, 43,* 4–9.

Young, N. (1989). Rockin' in the free world. On *Freedom* [audio CD]. WEA/Warner Brothers.

Young, N. (1994). Driveby [Recorded by Neil Young and Crazy Horse]. On *Sleeps with angels* [audio CD]. USA: Reprise Records.

Index

Francis J. Ryan, Ed.D. is Professor of Education and American Studies at La Salle University, where he teaches courses in foundations of education, social and moral development, American history, and American Studies. He has published in numerous journals and presented at national and international conferences. His current interests include the history of American education, American immigration and ethnicity, culture theory, and character education.

John J. Sweeder is Associate Professor of Education at La Salle University in Philadelphia, Pennsylvania, where he teaches courses in educational technology, secondary teacher education, and educational psychology. He received his Ed.D. in English/Communication education from Temple University. He has published widely in professional journals and presented at national and international conferences.

Maryanne R. Bednar is Associate Professor of Education at La Salle University in Philadelphia, Pennsylvania, where she teaches courses in reading, secondary education, assessment, and young adult literature. She received her Ph.D. in educational psychology with an emphasis on reading from Temple University. She has presented at numerous national and international conferences and published widely in professional journals.

Studies in the Postmodern Theory of Education

General Editors
Joe L. Kincheloe & Shirley R. Steinberg

Counterpoints publishes the most compelling and imaginative books being written in education today. Grounded on the theoretical advances in criticalism, feminism, and postmodernism in the last two decades of the twentieth century, Counterpoints engages the meaning of these innovations in various forms of educational expression. Committed to the proposition that theoretical literature should be accessible to a variety of audiences, the series insists that its authors avoid esoteric and jargonistic languages that transform educational scholarship into an elite discourse for the initiated. Scholarly work matters only to the degree it affects consciousness and practice at multiple sites. Counterpoints' editorial policy is based on these principles and the ability of scholars to break new ground, to open new conversations, to go where educators have never gone before.

For additional information about this series or for the submission of manuscripts, please contact:

Joe L. Kincheloe & Shirley R. Steinberg
c/o Peter Lang Publishing, Inc.
275 Seventh Avenue, 28th floor
New York, New York 10001

To order other books in this series, please contact our Customer Service Department:

(800) 770-LANG (within the U.S.)
(212) 647-7706 (outside the U.S.)
(212) 647-7707 FAX

Or browse online by series:

www.peterlangusa.com